DATE DUE

Concept Formation and Learning in Early Childhood

Dean R. Spitzer

CONCEPT FORMATION AND LEARNING IN EARLY CHILDHOOD

Dean R. Spitzer

University of North Carolina
at Wilmington

Charles E. Merrill Publishing Co.
A Bell & Howell Co.
Columbus, Ohio 43216

For Barbara

372.71
Sp 49c

Published by
Charles E. Merrill Publishing Co.
A Bell & Howell Co.
Columbus, Ohio 43216

This book was set in News Gothic and Olive Antique.
The production editor was Sandy Smith.
The cover was designed by Will Chenoweth.

Front cover photo bottom left by Julie Estadt.
All other cover photos by Steven G. Smith.

International Standard Book Number: 0-675-08553-5

Library of Congress Catalog Card Number: 76-24083

1 2 3 4 5 6 7 8 9 10—82 81 80 79 78 77

Printed in the United States of America

Preface

This book is intended primarily for preservice educators as well as parents and other adults concerned with helping individuals attain their fullest potential. Extensive evidence in recent years has indicated that there must be rich and exciting early experiences for young children if they are to develop all of their inherent abilities. Education is cumulative; rich experiences in later schooling depend upon the foundation that has been laid in early childhood. Equality of social and educational opportunity will never be a reality until this early foundation of experiences is equalized and expanded. This book aims at providing an integrated view of early childhood learning and suggests approaches for building the strongest possible foundation of early experiences upon which the child will be able to build.

The integrating core of this book is the notion of *concept formation,* the fundamental process through which humans *organize* their experiences into functional categories. The manner in which human beings are able to deal with and use all the information and stimuli that bombard them has been one of the great mysteries of psychological science. Forming concepts allows us to group experiences in the most efficient way. Furthermore, the early development of concept-like groupings of experiences appears to be the most significant single accomplishment of intellectual growth in early childhood. Most of this early learning revolves around basic perceptual experiences and exploration of the child's environment.

It is my belief that the more we know about the processes that shape our lives, the better equipped we will be to intervene in these processes in a positive way. However, there is a bewildering amount of literature on early childhood learning and education. This book was the result of a need on the part of the author and numerous others for a simple, comprehensive, and integrated approach to the issues involved. In addition, it was felt that there should be an approach that brought together both theory and practice in the same text.

Depending on the interests of the reader, this book can be read and appreciated at many different levels. The text is simply written and left relatively free from scholarly references. However, references are available at the end of the book as notes, and there is a comprehensive bibliography grouped according to subject. The hope is that the reader will be spurred on to further investigation of the original sources, having a comprehensive overview of the field.

An effort has been made to integrate a vast amount of theory and research, while also maintaining the unique spirit of each research and theoretical approach. Among the major lines of research which have been treated are developmental theories, learning theories, information-processing theories, and perception theories. Although these theoretical approaches are very different, they seem to reinforce each other surprisingly well.

This book is divided into two parts: the first part includes the background theory, research, and interpretation of this literature; the second part provides a compilation of activities which can be used to enrich the early experiences of young children. Theory and practice can, and should, be used simultaneously. Good theory and good practice should never be far apart.

I would like to take this opportunity to express my debt to all the researchers and educators who have been cited in this text. In a real sense this is their book as much as mine. As a result of the dedication of these researchers, from many different areas of social science, we have developed an exciting field of knowledge. It is now our responsibility to act upon this knowledge and continue the search for new truths. To my wife Barbara, words of thanks are not enough nor is the dedication of this book. Her hand is everywhere in inspiring this work and all my other efforts; she is, in a real sense, the co-author of everything I write, but she is too modest to take credit for it. Thanks are also due to Claudia Kirby for preparing the final manuscript and to Sandy Smith for her editorial assistance. Finally, thanks are due to the anonymous reviewers of the manuscript whose comments and suggestions improved this text immeasurably.

Contents

part 1   **THEORY**   **1**

  1   Introduction   2
  2   The Young Child in Society   8
  3   The Intellectual Development of the Child   16
  4   What Are Concepts?   23
  5   Learning and Concept Formation   29
  6   The Stages of Concept Formation   41
  7   Early Conceptual Experiences   49
  8   Early Learning Abilities   56
  9   Visual Concepts   66
10   Learning and Play   72
11   The Role of the Adult   78
12   Fostering Creativity   82
13   Motivation and Early Learning   92
14   Summary   97

part 2   **ACTIVITIES**   **99**

Introduction   100
Activities: Three Weeks to Five Months   106
Activities: Five Months to One Year   111
Activities: One Year to Five Years   117

Notes   150

References   160

Index   168

part 1

THEORY

1
Introduction

This book has been written to provide the reader with a mix between theory and practice, both of which are essential for any successful educational endeavor. Although the main text is purposely free from specific academic references, you will find theoretical explanations and references in the notes to each chapter, and there is a complete reference section. These sections list sources that have been specifically used in the writing of the text and those that have had a more indirect effect on the author's work. They are offered for the reader who wants to investigate topics further. The principal implications of the research that has most influenced the structure and content of the book are presented in this chapter.

Kurt Lewin, the famous social psychologist, has been quoted as saying, "There is nothing as practical as a good theory." A theory, by definition, permits us to view events in a more systematic and organized way and to predict the outcome of those events. The field of early childhood education is an area that needs good theory. There is so much information available. Thousands and thousands of research articles have been produced in recent years. It is indeed bewildering for the parent or teacher who wants to make sense of all this knowledge in a useful and practical way. This book aims at providing a bridge toward such a practical use of this research.

Importance of Early Experiences

The focus of this book is the first years of life. These are the years when independent exploration is so important. The infant is born with many potential abilities which too frequently are not fully realized. Therefore, the fundamental thesis of this book is the following: Provide the young child with some basic educational resources in a systematic and organized manner; maintain close supervision without stifling his creativity; provide the opportunity for the child to build his own conception of reality, exercising all his intellectual, perceptual, and motor abilities along the way, and the child will develop all of his potential and be ready to cope with the intellectual demands of life. In early education it seems that allowing a young child to do what he does best, explore, is most beneficial for him. This book stresses the activity of a young child and the nature of his early interaction with his environment. I believe that there is no greater adventure for adults and children than participating cooperatively in this extraordinary educational endeavor.

This book is concerned with the way a young child *experiences* his world, the manner in which he *perceives* it, the way he *manipulates* it, and the way he *organizes* it. The accent is on the power of the individual child to develop his own intellectual capacities, given a rich and supportive environment. Primary among these environmental influences is the perception-based experience that we so often tend to take for granted. These are the extremely rich sensory experiences that are difficult to repeat or replenish after the first years of life. They represent the basis of the *concepts of early childhood,* the foundation of experience with which we interpret subsequent experience. It is important that young children have a rich store of firsthand experience with the concrete aspects of their environment for, later in life, much experience becomes "secondhand," or vicarious. In terms of early childhood education, this means that we should concentrate on the most basic forms of early learning, and this is the learning that young children seem to benefit from most.

Theoretical Background

The theoretical background of this book is quite a mixed one. Literally thousands of researchers have contributed to the theory behind this book. Such an approach has been referred to by some as being "the best of all possible worlds" approach. Indeed, that is what the attempt has been: to integrate the diverse findings in the early childhood development and education literature and mold them into an organized and coherent whole. Although the major thrust of this approach is "developmental," there are many other influences prominent in the pages that follow. In essence, I have made an attempt to gather information that already exists in diverse sources and to unify and explain it so that a practical program for action emerges. The major research trends underlying the rationale for this book are as follows.

Early stimulation and environmental enrichment have extreme positive effects on the child's future performance.[1] There is a very large body of evidence which supports the belief that appropriate stimulation of the child in early life, particularly during the first three years, will have profound positive effects on future performance in school and in life.[2] This stimulation need not be specifically structured, but it should provide the child with a challenging environment in terms of variety of objects, visual sensations, activities, problems to solve, and new experiences to encounter. Research shows that unless a child receives adequate experience, especially in terms of sensory experience, his ability to deal with subsequent experiences throughout life will be detrimentally affected.[3]

Perceptual and sensory learning is the most efficient learning for young children.[4] During the first few years of life, children develop more than 90 percent of their ability to process visual information, and visual information alone accounts for almost 90 percent of all the information humans deal with in their lives.[5] The use of early perceptual training has proven successful in instances in which it has been used. The best training for sensory perception is simply the exposure of young children to a wide variety of perceptual experiences.[6] If these experiences do not occur early in life, they may not occur at all, since in later childhood there are developmental tasks that usually take preference over sensory learning, like language skills and social learning.[7]

Early learning is a direct function of experience.[8] Within certain limits, research has shown that young children do not need *specific* instruction in how to experience their world so much as they need the opportunity to test, practice, and elaborate the skills that they develop quite naturally through maturation.[9] New skills, no matter how naturally they are acquired, need practice to improve them and make them more functional in practical situations. The human senses are an ideal example. They develop naturally, and, perhaps because of this fact, they are all too often taken for granted; it is rarely recognized that our senses need exercise as much as our bodies do.[10]

The more experience a child has with the world, the more he wants.[11] This is similar to the notion that success breeds success. Experience is learning more about the world of people, objects, and events and is extremely pleasurable for the young child; the more he has, the more he wants.

The earlier in life that learning becomes associated with pleasure, the better. An additional advantage that seems to accrue from early experience is the linking of learning with pleasure. If the child is encouraged to explore, is given the appropriate means to do so, and continually achieves success, he will have highly pleasurable and rewarding results.[12] This pleasure is bound to transfer to other learning activities and will probably have a profound influence on attitudes toward future learning experiences.[13]

Concept formation is the fundamental basis of thought and the means by which we organize our diverse experience.[14] Concepts are the categories which human beings use to organize all the environmental stimuli which bombard their senses constantly. They help to give meaning to what would otherwise be chaotic experiences.[15] It is through concept formation that we use our past experience to organize present and future experience. Generally speaking, children who have formed the most efficient concepts and organization of knowledge will be most successful in school and in living.

Concepts lead to economy of learning.[16] Those who have the most success at learning are those who have had the opportunity to organize their existing knowledge and build upon it with subsequent experience. Some people learn the same things over and over in different ways, thus limiting the scope of their experiences. Concepts, in effect, make different experiences equivalent by allowing us to identify the similar elements of our experiences. This permits us to concentrate on those elements that are unique. In this way, concepts do lead to very efficient learning with a minimum of duplication and wasted effort.[17]

Early instruction on how to organize knowledge and the provision for a great variety of experiences will usually lead to the formation of the most useful concepts.[18] What research evidence there is, and admittedly there is not very much, indicates that basic concepts (perceptually oriented concepts) form naturally with adequate experience, and these early concepts form the basis of most subsequent learning. Children who have had the benefit of early experience are more able to organize information meaningfully and most frequently perform more efficiently than those who have been deprived of this early experience.

Appropriate early experiences lead the child to feelings of competence and self-effectiveness, which in turn lead to a well-developed self-concept and higher expectations of self.[19] If learning experiences are carefully monitored by the adult and are appropriate to the level of the learner (this can be seen very simply by observing the child's success), then the child will develop feelings of competence and mastery which will spur him on to more and better learning. If the child is having difficulty, simply move on to an activity which is more appropriate to his level of preparedness. There is no harm in testing activities to see if the child is ready for them. If you feel that a simpler activity is more appropriate, do not hesitate to use it. Research has conclusively shown that success breeds success and competence-motivation is a most powerful human drive.[20]

Perception is, to a large extent, a learned ability and is a type of concept formation.[21] Because the use of our senses is taken so much for granted, few take the time to explore and understand the mechanisms of perception, which are complex indeed. Perception is the process through which we "interpret" our experiences; it is more than just the reception of sensations. In a real sense, our experiences are no better than our perceptual interpretation of them.[22] The ability to perceive things efficiently is learned through experience, in much the same way that we form other concepts in order to organize knowledge.

Learning should become a joyful, natural, and continuing activity; and, as such, it requires the joint effort of adult and child. Almost everything humans can do becomes a vital and worthwhile learning experience. This is particularly true in the early years of life, when everything is so new and exciting. Researchers have found that an incredible amount of learning occurs both intentionally and unintentionally during the first five years of life. The more intentional this learning becomes, the better organized will be the child's experience and the more functional his concepts will become. This requires a cooperative effort on the part of the adult and child. As the adult becomes more aware of the nature of early childhood learning and the type of activities which are most effective in fostering it, cooperative learning will soon become second nature. The result will be joyful explorations of the world, explorations which will probably be as much of an eye-opener for the adult as for the child.

Vision is our most important sense, but all our senses are important in themselves and should not be ignored.[23] As mentioned earlier, about 90 percent of all perception and human information processing is visual. The efficiency of our other senses appears to be integrally related to effective vision. However, we will really not be able to understand the operation of our other senses unless we concentrate upon their unique features. Many of the activities in Part 2 are aimed at giving the young child one of the only chances he might ever have to experiment with his sensory capabilities, experiencing and exploring with senses other than vision.

Language acquisition should not be the central focus of early learning; it should be a means to communicate concerning more basic learnings.[24] We live in a verbally oriented society. So much of our learning is based upon language, and, unfortunately, so little of it is based on actual experience. It is particularly important for early experience to deal most directly with actual manipulation and exploration of the child's environment. Language is very important, and communication between adult and child should be encouraged, but language learning should not be an end in itself. It should be a means through which the child acquires more information about his world, learns to question it, and shares experiences more effectively with others. If we do encourage memorization of vocabulary at a very early age, language learning will probably come at the expense of more fundamental concrete experience and may rob the child of the sensory and perceptual learning which is so basic to future success.[25]

All learning is hierarchical in nature. There must develop a strong base for future learning, and this foundation of sensory and perceptual learning is the ideal learning of early childhood.[26] If learning is to be efficient and rewarding, it is necessary for knowledge to be based on previous, more basic information. The child who learns abstract information before he learns concrete information will probably become a less successful learner. The hierarchy of learning is like a cone of which sensory experience forms the foundation; more abstract information comes later. It is inefficient structural design to build the tower before the foundation; similarly it is poor instruction to teach the specifics before the basics.

This book is a hybrid approach to early childhood education, based on thorough reviews of the latest research evidence. It aims to do more than suggest effective methods for the intellectual development of the young child; it endeavors to indicate ways to develop a path toward efficient instruction and appropriate early learning, without dictating one way alone. It explores the nature of early intellectual development, based on the belief that concrete concepts are the foundation of all thought. This approach provides a firm foundation of knowledge upon which to formulate and evaluate procedures for the early stimulation of the child. Without this prerequisite knowledge, preschool activities can be little more than doing what you are told, and this type of activity will soon become standardized and static. The approach presented here demands the active participation of the adult, both parent and teacher, to provide a cooperative educational effort. Information and possible approaches are suggested; the rest is up to the reader.

Finally, it should be understood that, although carefully grounded upon research and theoretical findings, the information in this book is not intended to be construed as conclusive. There are many ideas that are new and different interpretations of the research. For example, there are numerous practical recommendations drawn from the observations of researchers. I would like to caution the reader from associating these applications too closely with the research from which they are derived. A certain "leap of faith" is necessary in drawing any practical implications from research and theory. This book is intended to be a contribution to the integration of theoretical and practical issues in child development and early education; it is not the final word. I hope the reader will bear this in mind.

2

The Young Child
in Society

Recently, early childhood has become a major area of social concern. In the 1960s emphasis on early education was spurred on by decades of research studies, great national affluence, and a realization that a significant segment of American society was losing out in the "education game." Although always important in individual families, the young child became the focal point of national attention. Head Start, Home Start, new nursery schools, Montessori, day care, follow through, Bereiter-Englemann, "Sesame Street," and many more programs came upon the scene. National news magazines picked up the cause; researchers began work with new inspiration, new vigor, and new funds. Books on new child-rearing practices and books on early intellectual development inundated the market. The late 1960s were definitely the years of the "preschool child."

In the 1970s, we find that a measure of equilibrium has been restored. Early childhood is still important, but it has lost some of its initial glory. Advocates of many exciting new programs have gone home to do more research. The number of books and articles on the subject has diminished considerably. The realities of our scarce research dollars have dampened some enthusiasm, and general economic austerity has reached most every home in the nation. Perhaps this is not so bad. Now is the time for retrospection and careful consideration of the nature and importance of early childhood in overall child development. How can we make the lives of our children more meaningful and prepare them for the demands of adult life? How can we find the right programs for the people who need them?

Background on Early Education

Concern over the importance of the early years of life is nothing new. Researchers and practitioners have been attempting to improve and extend early childhood educational opportunities for many years. Maria Montessori began her prolific work with young children around the turn of the century in her native Italy. She recognized that young children need the opportunity to explore and manipulate their environment, above and beyond the opportunities that are normally permitted the young child. More than any other single individual, Montessori has probably been responsible for much of our increased awareness of the needs of young children.[1] Although her work has been primarily practical, her programs have stimulated a great deal of research. Indeed, Maria Montessori was the pioneer of early childhood education and training long before this field had become fashionable. Montessori experimented with materials that allowed young children to have structured experiences with novel items, which would be both developmentally sound and perceptually exciting. Today, her early experiments have been refined considerably, and her schools have spread throughout the world.

The theoretical groundwork for early childhood educational programs has been laid through the extensive research activities of a number of giants in the field. The names of Nancy Bayley, Arnold Gesell, Louise Ames, Lois Murphy, Jerome Kagan, Jean Piaget, Peter Wolff, Robert Fantz, Jerome Bruner, Eleanor Gibson, J. McV. Hunt, Rene Spitz, Benjamin Bloom, Burton White, Ira Gordon, Lev Vygotsky, Donald Hebb (to name but a few) will live in the history books for their detailed contributions to our knowledge of child development.[2] A compendium of references from these important studies is provided in the bibliography of this book. It is highly recommended to the reader to take the time to look through some of these original studies in order to understand the research basis for existing enrichment programs for young children. There is no substitute for viewing actual research, although reading such work is frequently difficult and tedious.

There are literally thousands of research articles concerned with the early childhood years in journals, such as *Child Development, Monographs of the Society for Research in Child Development, Journal of Experimental Child Psychology, Journal of Child Psychiatry, Journal of Comparative and Physiological Psychology, Journal of Genetic Psychology, Psychological Bulletin, American Psychologist, Psychological Review, American Journal of Psychology, Science, Merrill-Palmer Quarterly, Developmental Psychology,* and the list goes on and on.[3] The knowledge that has been produced through these studies has been extensive. However, putting together all this information in terms of practical responses to issues in child development has been less than we might have hoped. The situation might be described as an overabundance and an underutilization.

Child development organizations also have spread rapidly. Many of these associations have attempted with some success to make practical sense of the prolific research. There are the American Association of Elementary-Kindergarten-Nursery Educators, the Association for Childhood Education International, the Child Study Association of America, the National Association for the Education of Young Children, the National Education Association, the National Kindergarten Association, Parent Cooperative Preschools International, and numerous other national and local organizations.[4] There are symposiums, meetings, and other contacts among concerned researchers, teachers, and parents.

Preschool Programs

Along with the rapid growth of early childhood education has come an increased awareness of the context of early childhood and an augmented social conscience. Nothing has served to stimulate interest in the early childhood years as much as the recognition that early deprivation of experience could hinder the young child's development throughout life. The research had been accumulating for years and years, but it was primarily the new American conscience that brought this evidence into the public eye. Part of the civil rights movement and the War on Poverty was the attempt to bring youngsters from relatively poor environments into compensatory programs. The main thrust of this major project was Head Start, a program designed to assist young children and their families to develop more of the potential that is present in every young child.[5] This would be accomplished through offering compensatory training, augmenting the sense of dignity and self-worth of both children and parents, and providing some early intellectual and social opportunities that most middle-class children take for granted. The well-funded program began in 1965 and excited the imagination of the nation. It is no exaggeration to say that it was the most ambitious preschool program ever attempted.

Head Start was more than just a compensatory preschool education project; it was a significant outcome of social ferment. According to Maya Pines, "Head Start is a desperate, last-minute attempt to make up for deficiencies not in the child, but in the educational system."[6] This is an apt description of the main motivation for the program. Research had been discovering that, to a considerable degree, what goes into the educational system comes out of it. In other words, if children begin school with severe developmental and learning deficiencies, they will probably come out of their scholastic careers in the same way, having gotten less than other children out of almost every educational experience. This information was a real shocker to a society that was priding itself on its new emphasis on egalitarianism. As Pines further explains, "It is too little, and much too late."[7] Indeed, as we assess the effects of Project Head Start, we find the results have not been tremendously encouraging, and few vestiges of the multimillion dollar program remain. However, maybe the indirect effects of the Head Start idea are more significant, in the long run, than the direct effects.

Perhaps Head Start did not fail; perhaps it was a success in terms of promoting the importance of the young child in society. It stimulated the imagination; it brought knowledge about child development to those who did not have it; it increased general awareness about the need for intervention in early development; and it provided the basis for many offshoots.

Following the introduction of Head Start, other programs made their appearance on the early childhood scene; many of them, federally funded. The Perry Preschool Project in Ypsilanti, Michigan, combined both school-based and at-home enrichment.[8] Projects in the New York City Schools sponsored by the Institute for Developmental Studies gained widespread support. The Bereiter-Englemann Program aimed at providing preschool children with specific cognitive skills that would facilitate their performance in formal schooling.[9] Generally speaking, most of these preschool projects were successful in raising measured I.Q. scores, but there was considerable doubt as to the long-term effects of such programs.[10] Educators know for a fact that short-term gains are easy to come by; yet it is difficult to explore whether these improvements are enduring. If we are to draw generalizations from these experimental programs, a primary one would have to be that, in the short run at least, early childhood educational programs tend to raise measured I.Q. significantly regardless of the specific nature of the program. However, whether these gains endure is problematical. One thing that seems to be assured is that, unless this intervention continues in the home, there is little hope for lasting results. All learning requires practice, and practice can best be accomplished in the home. Unfortunately, there is little research concerned with the combined effects of in-school and at-home intervention projects, especially because controlled research in the home is virtually impossible.

Progress in preschool projects has been spurred on by some prominent advocates of such programs, most of them researchers in their own right. J. McV. Hunt has said, "The problem for the management of child development is to find out how to govern the encounters that children have with their environments to foster both an optimally rapid rate of intellectual development and a satisfying life."[11] William Fowler, who is particularly well-known for his efforts to teach his preschool daughter to read, has added, "In no instance (where documentation exists) have I found any individual of high ability who did not experience intensive early stimulation as a central component of his development."[12] Additional ammunition was added by the publication of Benjamin Bloom's influential review of the relevant research on human development *Stability and Change in Human Characteristics* in 1964.[13] In his book Bloom stresses the need for early experience, since certain limits of intelligence and perceptual abilities are determined before entrance to formal schooling. Although acutely aware of the limitations of existing studies, Bloom points out that certain limits on intelligence, growth, and perceptual abilities appear to be set by the age of five.[14]

Jean Piaget's Influence

Certainly the rediscovery of the work of Jean Piaget, discussed at length later in this book, added a great deal of practical evidence to the existing stock of knowledge concerning child development. During the 1960s, newly translated versions of the great Swiss psychologist's work began to emerge. Although most of his work was done prior to 1960, it was not until the awakening of this new interest in the preschool child that his monumental studies became well-known to the layman. In addition to translations of his work, there have been many interpretations of his findings.[15] Today, there is no more important name in child psychology than Piaget, and his influence will probably endure forever. His studies of his own children, detailing almost every action in response to structured stimulation, are incredible works of observational research. Although I would hardly recommend his original studies for the general reader, it is valuable to take a glimpse at his meticulous observations simply for their historical importance.

Educational Television

Perhaps nothing has excited public opinion more than the advent of preschool educational television. Programs like "Captain Kangaroo" have been on television for more than twenty years, going about their quiet, but effective, business of exposing young children to a greater variety of experiences. However, the major excitement in television programming for young children came with the development of "Sesame Street" by the Children's Television Workshop, premiering in 1969.[16] This program, which continues to be one of the most successful preschool enterprises ever, aims at "selling" education to preschoolers in the same fashion that products are sold to them in between cartoons on Saturday mornings. It surpassed all expectations in terms of measurable learning. Children loved it, learned from it, and extended their experience from it. How could anyone find fault with such a lofty enterprise? Although no one would criticize the Children's Television Workshop, "Sesame Street" has apparently caused some concern in early childhood education circles. Originally, this heavily funded effort was intended primarily as a compensatory program for less-privileged youngsters. It was hoped that children who could not avail themselves of other preschool opportunities would be stimulated by "Sesame Street," which stressed mostly verbal skills, thus increasing school entry skills. However, largely because of its educational television designation, it was shown on UHF educational stations. Due to the lack of UHF adaptors on television sets in inner-city areas and parents' lack of familiarity with educational television programming alternatives, a great majority of children who watched "Sesame Street" were from already more privileged backgrounds. The result was that the rich tended to get richer, and the poor relatively poorer. This, however, is in no way intended to derogate the important contribution that "Sesame Street" has made. More than anything else, perhaps, this revolutionary program brought the importance of early childhood education to the forefront of the public's educational concerns.

Meanwhile, there has been an awakened awareness of the social context of early childhood. For example, there has been a reaction against the cartoon-dominated fare of commercial television aimed at young children. Such groups as Action for Children's Television have become rather vocal advocates of programming improvement. Other groups have begun to call for the end of televised violence during hours that young children tend to watch television. There has been a new distinction made between "prosocial" and "antisocial" television programming influences.[17] Little evidence exists, however, showing a direct link between antisocial behaviors and television content. The closest that researchers have come to such a relationship has been findings that children with already existing aggressive tendencies can be made more so through constant observation of the violent actions of others. But, for the normal child, the relationship does not appear to be very strong.

New Social Context

There is little doubt that young children today live in a totally new social context than children of twenty, even ten, years ago. Children are inundated with already-packaged, secondhand experiences. Manufacturers have realized that toys and games for young children are very big business. Educational and noneducational toys proliferate everywhere, and thorough advertising campaigns proclaim the merits of each. Television itself has added an entirely new dimension to childhood. There is no doubt that young children are more aware and knowledgeable than children of earlier generations. Children today have so many information-rich experiences that it is hard to believe that these do not have a profound effect upon their development. Unfortunately, it is really too soon to reliably interpret the research that is currently underway concerning this issue. What evidence there is seems to indicate that children are acquiring extraordinary amounts of information without having the opportunity to use it. One of the primary tenets of this book is that young children desperately need active, manipulative experiences. This type of experience seems, in many cases, to take second place to secondhand experiences (vicarious experiences), such as television. Furthermore, children just don't seem to have the intellectual tools to deal with this vicarious experience.

It is really quite easy for children to go through their early years without having very much self-initiated experience. I have heard of some youngsters who watch television from a very early age, play entirely with toys which have been programmed for their use by manufacturers, and have parents who are not really attentive because they are just too busy. I have a feeling that these children will miss a great deal of early childhood and develop fewer of their potentials. Our consumer-oriented society gives us many conveniences, but child development can be short-circuited by "labor-saving devices." We just have not found adequate replacements for allowing the natural curiosity of children to run its course, and there is no substitute for the loving care, affection, and concern of the parent.

However, we must be aware of the trends in society that will change the environment in which children will live. Change is occurring so fast today that it is most difficult to keep pace, much less predict. There are certain developments which seem assured. For example, we seem to be moving from a predominantly *verbal* culture to a much more *visual* one. Television has had a lot to do with this transition, as Caleb Gattegno explains so well in his excellent book *Toward a Visual Culture.*[18] Elementary school teachers are even today acutely aware of this situation, and they ask, "Why can't Johnny read?" Indeed, the verbal abilities of young children seem to be increasing less rapidly than their visual abilities. There are many who advocate a reversal of this trend, but most acknowledge a change in our cultural values as the primary stimulus for this situation, and cultural values are difficult to change. I think that we will have to accept the importance of visual communication for today's young people, and help them continue to develop these abilities without sacrificing their verbal skills.[19] This will involve the development of sophisticated new programs. It will also require the concerted effort of both parents and teachers. If children are going to obtain much of their information from the visual media, they will have to learn to *interpret* and *use* this information more intelligently. Much of this book is concerned with the development of these abilities in their primitive aspects.

Early education has been, in large measure, shaped by big government and big business. There have been major successes and major failures. We know a tremendous amount about child development, but still very little about the ways children learn. We have a pretty good idea that much of child development occurs naturally through normal maturation. However, as a result of decades of research, we know that early stimulation does make a profound difference. We also know that perceptual abilities, the abilities that relate to our intake of information from our environment, will become more and more important. This book is intended to help develop an awareness of the processes and activities that researchers have found to be vital to successful development for today's society and the society we see emerging in the future. The challenge of child development is an exciting one, but one that must be engaged in from a position of knowledge and strength, not from ignorance and weakness. This chapter has endeavored to provide a social context for what follows.

3

The Intellectual Development of the Child

Not long ago there was widespread support for the belief that intelligence was a fixed quantity, based wholly on hereditary factors. It used to be widely accepted that a person's intelligence would run its predetermined course naturally.[1] Today there is much evidence to refute the notion of fixed intelligence, although we realize that there are certain psychological limits which are probably determined in large part by inheritance.[2] Considerable variance, which can be attributed to experience and experience-related factors, is possible in intellectual development. Given two children with reasonably similar inherited intelligence, the child with the richer and more varied experience will, all other factors being equal, develop faster and farther than the other child. There is little we can do about heredity, but there is much we can do in accelerating the extent and rate of the intellectual development of children, especially during the first few years of life.

Although there is considerable agreement among authorities that intelligence is only in part predetermined, there is general acknowledgment that development does occur in a standard order.[3] This is the belief in stages of development, an idea that certain developmental events must come before others. There is ample evidence that development occurs in a fixed sequence, although the length of these sequential stages may vary considerably from individual to individual, depending upon many factors. The principal determinant of the nature of these stages of development seems to be the richness of the young child's environment.[4]

The organization of this chapter will follow the system of developmental stages outlined by Piaget. Some of the information presented is derived from his meticulous researches. However, the material presented is not intended to be totally consistent with his findings and integrates evidence from numerous other researchers and educators. Our consistent references to Piaget's work attest to his contribution. More than anyone else, he has been responsible for the rebirth of popular interest in the important early childhood years. Furthermore, his structuring of the stages of development is the foundation upon which most early childhood theorizing is built. Piaget's clinical, or observational, method of viewing early development is a wonder of psychological science. Anyoné interested in delving deeper into the subject is recommended to go to the original work of this master.

Piaget's Theory

One of the most significant observations in early childhood educational research is Piaget's remark, "The intelligence organizes the world by organizing itself."[5] This statement is quite representative of the philosophy behind Piaget's work, with its emphasis on the importance of the child's own actions. According to him, intelligence is not passive but develops through the active participation of the learner. Intelligence develops as the child begins to come to grips with his environment. In his explanation of the nature of the development of intelligence, Piaget describes two complementary *adaptive* processes: assimilation and accommodation. It is through these processes that the child learns to deal effectively with his environment; really, this is intelligence.

Assimilation and Accommodation

Assimilation is the process through which children acquire information from the environment and incorporate this information into existing knowledge. *Accommodation* is the process through which children revise their existing knowledge in order to satisfy the requirements of the environment. Both of these processes are instrumental to early development of intelligence. Derived from Piaget's study of biology, these processes are quite natural developments. Assimilation aids children in extending their knowledge and awareness, while accommodation provides the mechanism for fitting this new knowledge to the constraints of the environment. For example, consider someone who is just learning to drive. This person has learned that the car will start by turning the key and pressing down the accelerator. Then, putting the car into gear and giving it gas will cause it to move forward. This information has been *assimilated* by the novice driver. However, this learning is not enough. The new driver also must learn, sometimes through bitter experience, that there are constraints, such as staying on the proper side of the road and paying attention to traffic signals and signs, that require him to behave in a certain controlled fashion. In other words, he must learn to *accommodate* to certain constraints. In essence, the same procedure is operational in most children's early learning experiences. There are always new things to learn, but there are also environmental contexts in which this new learning must fit.

    Young children are voracious learners, constantly exploring and learning. However, it is not enough that they learn new information; they must also learn to use this information. In a very real sense, early learning is active learning, and new information must be put to use. Examples of active learning through assimilation and accommodation abound. Perhaps one of the easiest examples to observe is the situation in which a child is beginning to understand the full significance of a ball. The child may watch the ball bouncing near him and follow its movements with great interest and anticipation. When the ball comes within his reach, he may try to grasp it. Then, there begins the lengthy process through which the child must accommodate his actions to the desire to grasp the ball. He must fit his perceptions of the ball to the real-life task of grasping it. He cannot just pick it up; he must form new motor responses for dealing with the task. Through *assimilation,* the child learns of the nature of the ball—its size, color, form, and other characteristics. Through *accommodation,* he learns more actively how to deal with this new stimulus. These two complementary processes occur constantly in early learning, and it is fascinating to view the child's actions in this context. In Piaget's developmental theory, all learning occurs as a result of these two complementary processes. Within reasonable limits, the more the child is made to adapt to new things in his environment, the more rapid and complete will be his intellectual growth.[6]

Stages of Development

Piaget describes four stages of the child's intellectual development: the *sensorimotor stage* (from birth to eighteen months), the *preoperational stage* (from eighteen months to about seven years), the *concrete-operational stage* (from about seven years to about eleven years), and the *formal-operational stage* (from about eleven years on). This chapter primarily will be concerned with the first two stages of development in which the child begins to develop the basic foundation of thought and the framework for his conceptual processes.

During the sensorimotor stage, the infant is engaged in his first environmental investigations. His world is at once strange, new, frightening, and exciting. At first these explorations are accomplished with the eyes only, as the infant does not yet have sufficient control of his body responses. During his next few months, the child is only able to direct his eyes toward light, objects, and people who intrude into his visual field. He is not yet able to explore actively on his own. Only very familiar things are clearly focused in the infant's vision, and his world is severely limited. Objects and people who leave his visual field are "gone" in the child's mind; they have disappeared. The newborn infant does not follow things with his eyes to discover where they are going.

Between three and six months, the child begins to explore with his eyes more actively. He is able to adapt to the forms of a greater variety of objects and to focus his eyes on them. He begins to follow objects more closely and develops an ability to recognize familiar things and respond to them. The child also begins to develop some control over his body movements and explores with his hands, as well as his eyes. He is only beginning to develop a concept of "object permanence."[7] That is, he can follow an object outside his immediate field of vision but cannot figure out what has happened to an object which has been hidden, even if it has been hidden while he watched.

The age of six months represents a significant milestone. At this time, the child begins to develop a considerable degree of control over his body movements. Object permanence is rapidly developing, and with it comes a more stable reality and the security the young child needs. He is beginning to distinguish between means and ends and to pursue simple goals. Piaget views the time between six and eight months as the point of origin of true intelligence, as the child has developed the ability to actively accommodate to his environment.[8] At this stage, the child is highly egocentric; he believes that the world revolves only around him. He recognizes that there are inexplicable things happening outside; they excite his curiosity and imagination. One of the first adaptive processes of the infant is imitation of people and things around him. Piaget sees this as the beginning of symbolic thought, and the precursor of language.

It is important to remember about this first half of the sensorimotor stage that the child is just beginning to leave the period of complete egocentrism, or complete concern with self. At this level, he still has great difficulty separating his subjective impressions from an objective reality, although the development of object permanence is an important step in this direction. The child is involved in much "feeling," but not "thinking" or "knowing"; he has some hunches about reality, but few substantial facts. As a result of increasing ability to move about and use other senses besides sight, the child is able to explore things in greater detail. His concentration increases, and he is able to undertake more prolonged and meaningful environmental investigations. This is an ideal time to begin to program more variety and enrichment in the child's environment.

At about twelve months, the child begins to develop new methods of exploration and discovery. He has finally mastered the concept of object permanence and can find an object which has been fully hidden. He is developing increased motor coordination; he can move himself around with ease and can explore actively when permitted. Play and imitation increase, and together they merge into what Piaget calls "symbolic play"; that is, the child is able to symbolically "act out" events he observes.[9] Symbolic play allows the child to think using actions. Thought is really the mental image of past experience; symbolic play is the "acting out" of past experience. Imitation, symbolic play, and fantasy are extremely important and creative processes at this stage of development.

At around eighteen months of age, the child leaves the sensorimotor period. He is no longer tied wholly to the present and what he sees immediately before him.[10] He is developing a usable store of past experience and is able to act upon it. He is also developing the ability to perceive the effects of actions and to attribute causes to them, even if the cause is not within his field of vision. He begins to be conscious of future time, and he is willing to defer gratification to some extent. Perhaps most important, the serious work of language development begins.

Everything new the child develops during this extraordinary period requires exercise. He should be given an enriched environment and encouragement for his physical, sensory, and mental explorations. Moreover, everything new the child comes in contact with will probably expand his ability to accommodate his environment. *Optimal growth depends upon a proper match between readiness and objects encountered.* As Piaget says of this stage of child development, "Sensorimotor intelligence acts like a slow motion film in which all the pictures are seen in succession, but without fusion and so without continuous vision necessary for understanding the whole."[11]

During the preoperational stage, from eighteen months to approximately seven years, the child develops most of the practical intellectual abilities that he will use later. He learns to use language and to categorize on the basis of concrete evidence, and he loses many of the egocentric behaviors that have prevented him from becoming a social being. This stage is marked by more active and consistent exploration of the environment. The child must be allowed to explore as much as possible. This is required for successfully adapting to the environment that Piaget emphasizes.

By the age of 2½ years, the child is more actively trying to organize his world through early conceptual groupings of experience. However, he is also prone to numerous contradictions and inconsistencies. He may not be able to recognize the nature of similarity and may be confused that similar objects are not the same object. The child might not be able to recognize that groups of objects compose larger entities. For example, he might not be able to understand that a town is composed of many separate houses and buildings together. He might see a cow and confuse this four-legged creature with a dog. The child is not yet ready to grasp the notion of similarity; he is prone to the misinterpretation that is caused by overreliance on perceptual characteristics or appearance.[12] The confusions and questions that result from this period show that the child is actively trying to piece together what he observes. This is a vitally important period of transition. The world of the child is growing at leaps and bounds, but the intellectual powers to deal with the increasing diversity still need to catch up.

Adults should take a very active role in this period of the child's development. Questions will come at a rapid rate and at unpredictable times. The child needs support and guidance in helping him try to explain the mass of confusion to which he is beginning to be exposed. The best thing to do is to encourage the child to ask questions and to help him find the answers. Just answering questions is not what the child needs; he needs help to find the answers himself. The child is trying to make the first major step in concept formation; yet it is still too soon for major advances in this area. He finds a problem in recognizing the difference between *similarity, equality,* and *separateness.* The idea of *class equivalence,* the fundamental notion of concept formation, is still a distance away. But it is through the child's own actions that this development must come.[13]

The child is rapidly accumulating the associative skills which he will soon use to form more sophisticated models of his widening world and reality. This is the time when a great variety of *organized* experience is so vital. This is also the time when close parental supervision can help the child come to grips with his world. However, the distinction should be made between *guidance* and *leadership.* The child needs to make the major advances himself; he does not need the parent to lead him to his understandings. He needs support, organization, and encouragement. He needs his questions to be answered in ways that will guide him to his own answers.

The child is also developing a substantial vocabulary, and his language is becoming adequately formed for social communication purposes. He continues to explore avidly and imitates the examples available to him. He is developing an increasing store of past experiences with which to evaluate present and future experiences.[14] He can increasingly differentiate between cause and effect and can more readily anticipate the effects of his actions. Increasing contradictions between perceptions add a new dimension to accommodation, and the child gradually learns to objectively explain inconsistencies between observations.

The most basic example of the contradictory nature of early childhood dependency upon perceptual evidence is the failure of the child to deal with *conservation* tasks.[15] This is frequently demonstrated by an experiment employing a short, round container and a tall, thin one. The same liquid is transferred back and forth from container to container. The child is asked which container has the most liquid, and, ruled by his concrete perceptions, he normally answers that the taller container has the most liquid because the liquid level is higher. The child cannot realize that both containers hold the same amount of liquid; the only difference is that one container is taller and the other is wider. The child knows what *wideness* and *tallness* are, but he cannot put them together. Tallness is seen more clearly than wideness because it is more immediately obvious, and the child has probably had more experience with it. *Higher* has become synonymous with *more*. According to Piaget, it will not be until the end of the preoperational stage, perhaps around the age of seven, that the child will be able to solve this important puzzle. Conservation of quantity (volume) is a prime example of what Piaget called "operational thought." It is through a gradual process of intellectual development that the child is freed from dependency on what he sees. Gradually, he develops the ability to *abstract* properties from what is directly observed.

Through this process, the child begins to understand that everything is composed of parts and properties, even if these properties (or attributes) are not directly observable. This is the realization that attributes of items can exist independently of those specific items, such as roundness, or tallness, or wideness. The child also becomes aware of the interrelationships between properties, such as the trade-off between tallness and wideness in the conservation task described above.

This description of the intellectual development of the young child has been brief. Great care should be taken to view it in its proper context. It is by no means exhaustive, and it is not a "rule." There is no reason why children cannot develop faster than the stages described here. Some children develop faster than others; some children develop in "spurts"; but usually the later bloomers catch up, sometimes even overtaking the earlier developers. The rate of development is not nearly as important as the extent of development. Child development is not a footrace. The quality of the process is much more significant to ultimate performance. That is why the emphasis in this book is on the qualitative aspects of each stage of growth. The idea is to provide as rich a basis as possible for each stage, in order to assure that each stage has been adequately formed and that learnings have been consolidated.

4

What Are Concepts?

Concepts are the mental tools we develop to help us cope with our complex world. They help us to order and simplify the tremendous variety of objects, people, and events that constantly compete for our attention. Concepts are very simply groups of things that we give common names. They are our way of making different things the same by treating them as part of the same category. Almost every noun or adjective is a verbal designation of a concept. Trees all look different, but we tend to treat them as the same things. There are infinite shades of the color red, and yet we tend to treat all reds as equivalent. We refer to the moon as round when it is full, and yet rarely is it perfectly round. We tend to think of a certain type of building as being a house, but sometimes it serves other purposes. These are just a few very elementary examples of how we use concepts to simplify our environment. We cannot afford to think of everything as unique and still be able to live our lives efficiently. Therefore, we must group our experience into categories, or else we would have to investigate everything separately and rarely would get anything accomplished.

Adults tend to take concept groupings for granted, after all they are the result of years and years of experience. However, the young child does not have this experience to draw on. Perhaps the major intellectual function of early childhood is the formation of concepts in order to allow the child to deal most efficiently with a world in which everything is totally new.

Concepts Are Functional

Think for a minute about all the unique experiences the world has to offer. Think about how utterly impossible it would be to experience everything as unique and different. One interesting example of how humans form useful concepts is by treating people according to their social "roles." For instance, we tend to treat a police officer as we would any other police officer, a salesperson in a store as we would any other salesperson, and the bus driver as we would any other bus driver. In effect, we have formed people concepts that allow us to deal with those people most efficiently.

Another practical example of the necessity of concept formation is in the supermarket. What a horror it would be if products were not classified into categories! If products were just randomly distributed throughout the store, it might take weeks to find items on a shopping list. As a consequence of this possibility, products are categorized so that it is easy to find the desired items. Essentially, the store manager is forming product-concepts for us. For example, within the product classification *cleansers* are all different types of products which serve roughly the same purpose—they clean. Consequently, concepts are, by definition, *functional*.[1] They help us organize our complex experiences and make the world more meaningful to us in our daily lives.

Our mental concepts help us organize our experiences much the same way as these physical arrangements help us find the things we want and need. Research findings indicate that the people who have formed the most functional concepts are able to live their lives most efficiently.[2] Combined, our concepts give us a rather stable foundation for dealing with our everyday lives and our environment. They help us organize our experiences and communicate them to others. Words are an example of the concepts we use for communication. We talk about a *tree* because people understand that word concept, where they might not understand specific references to a *bonsai*. We talk of *freedom* and *democracy* as if they were the same conditions in every case, because we must simplify the real world for the sake of efficient communication. In brief, concepts represent the organized synthesis of all our learning.

External and Internal Concepts

In understanding concepts and classification, we should be aware of two general types, *external* and *internal*.[3] External concepts are those that have been imposed upon us, like library and supermarket schemes, by people seeking to simplify our lives. Internal concepts are those that we manufacture ourselves to help us deal with the complexity of our own experiences. We should recognize when our environment is being organized for us and when we have to do it ourselves. It is an interesting exercise to think of the many ways others have organized our lives, from the supermarket to urban planning to governmental supervision. Our experience has been classified, and, to a degree, programmed, by regulations, architecture, planning, landscaping, and hundreds of other processes. But just as urban planning, governmental regulation, and architectural design are creative activities used by others for functionally grouping our experiences, so are the internal concepts that we develop ourselves. The creative nature of concept formation should always be understood, appreciated, and admired.

Limitations of Concepts

There are, however, possible penalties for grouping our experiences into concepts, for we are essentially trading uniqueness for efficiency. Through concept formation, or *conceptualization,* we are streamlining our experiences, but perhaps also limiting them. In placing a tree into the conceptual category *tree*, we are actually saying that such wooden things with tree-like characteristics *are equivalent* for purposes of classification. For our everyday purposes, this is rarely a handicap, but we should be aware that there is a trade-off between concepts and unique experiences. An artist, for example, must look at his experiences differently than the average person. He must look for things, and unique aspects of things, with an eye for the novel and different. His stock-in-trade is his interpretation of unique aspects of his environment. Our ordinary experiences cannot usually tolerate this type of view. We must live our lives by dealing with classes of things, rather than treating everything as unique. However, this does not mean that the average person cannot sometimes experience things in the same way that an artist does. Just because we need to operate with efficiency in dealing with our daily tasks does not mean that we cannot learn to appreciate the uniqueness of specific aspects of our world. Unfortunately, children are seldom taught this ability. The development of rich and diverse concepts can afford children an opportunity to determine on what level they wish to experience their world. We can all be artists sometimes and efficient shoppers other times.

Organizing Children's Experiences

We all conceptualize; we all develop classification systems, because the complexity of our lives demands it. Still, there are serious choices and decisions which can and must be made regarding concept formation, and the most important decisions should deal with how we structure our children's experiences in order to enrich their concepts. The principal question is, How should we help our children develop concepts which will make their lives most efficient, while still maximizing their appreciation of all that is unique and wonderful in their environment and everyday world?

There are very definite, learned mental mechanisms which control the way we conceptualize. Research evidence shows that these patterns of mental development occur very early in a child's life and are usually very much a part of preschool experiences.[4] In our first months and years we learn to come to grips with our environment, to explore, to manipulate, and we begin to classify. In these first few remarkable years the patterns of our intellectual development are formed, and these follow us through to adulthood.[5] It is not that these patterns are irreversible but that we get into habits which seem to reinforce each other and, consequently, do not change. Piaget has said that concepts form the very basis of all thought and the basis of most intelligent activity.[6] *The importance of early conceptualization should be carefully understood by parents and teachers so that these opportunities for intellectual growth are fully utilized.*

Language Acquisition

The extreme significance of early conceptual development can better be studied and understood through the consideration of language acquisition, the formation of the most common type of concept—words. Words are the basic elements of language, but they are too often misunderstood. Our society puts a tremendous emphasis on the acquisition of a large vocabulary in young children. But few realize that words without experience are meaningless. They are but empty concepts. Language allows humans to communicate meaningfully with others. The more experience and meaning that backs up words, the more rewarding the communication process will become.

It should be understood that the newborn child comes into the world with no prior knowledge of people, objects, and events; everything must be learned. All children have an instinctive desire to communicate, and they will learn to do so soon enough without having to be drilled at learning meaningless words. In order for a child to develop a foundation of meaningful early concepts, she must learn through actual concrete experience. There is so much to do and learn in these early years that we should try to make this learning as meaningful and organized for the child as we can. We must make certain that the words and other concepts the child learns are backed up by experience and knowledge; as such, the information will become extremely functional and meaningful. Knowledge without concrete meaning can become a source of frustration for the young child. Early education must be experientially oriented, and it is easy for us to do so. There is a wealth of knowledge available and endless numbers of wonderful things in the environment of every home with which to stimulate the child. There are objects of different colors and textures;

there are art works, sculptures, photographs; there are materials which we adults take for granted but which the imagination of children needs for stimulation and practice in the use of language and the formation of concepts.

It is impossible to expose the child to every experience and every instance of every concept. However, it is possible to expose her to as great a variety of environmental stimuli as possible, and there is every indication that this *variety of experience* is the most valuable thing a parent or teacher can give a child in these very early stages of development. It is through these varied experiences that language and thought are given meaning. The more concrete experiences that back up every word and mental image, the richer the base will be on which the child has to build. Outward facility with language and a large vocabulary can hide a lack of understanding. When a child learns a word, she is learning a concept that might represent thousands of separate experiences and that might have room for thousands more. It is *the cumulative significance of these experiences* that gives a word or other concept its meaning. *Meaning is the ultimate content of concepts,* as interpreted by the individual.[7] It is continually changing and is reinterpreted as the individual adds new experiential evidence.

Meaning cannot be taken for granted, for it is the very substance of all learning. Language is nonsense without meaning. Where vocabulary is the quantitative dimension of language, meaning is the qualitative dimension. We take this latter dimension for granted and frequently measure language acquisition on the basis of vocabulary only. This is a serious error. Language is not like walking and breathing, as Edward Sapir points out in his influential book *Language*.[8] There is nothing innate in the individual which causes language to develop; it derives largely from the need of people to communicate in a social context. Depending upon our experiences with the environment, some of us have deeper and richer meanings attached to our verbal symbols than others. Perhaps the greatest beauty of language is that it allows people to share all these different experiences. Meaning is a reflection and facilitator of experience. The deeper the meaning that lies behind our language, the more substantial our communication will be with others, as well as all subsequent experiences.

There is also another type of meaning in language; this is the meaning provided by context. Just as many aspects of our environment are shaped for us, so too are aspects of our language shaped by other people and society. The way people speak, their emphasis, the emotional overtones, the expressive aspects of the voice add a sort of "hidden meaning" to words. A child with very limited experiences upon which to base language meaning is particularly susceptible to these hidden meanings.

The parent or teacher whose vocal inflections frighten the young child may instill unpleasant associations for certain words. Enthusiasm can leave the child with very positive feelings.

Language is one of the most important human learnings. Through rich and varied experiences we achieve meaning for the words we use. *Seasons* may mean simply fall, spring, summer, and winter to one person, while it may have extraordinarily vivid experiences associated with it to another. Autumn leaves, pumpkins, magnificent colors for fall; cold, icicles, snowballs, bare but beautiful trees for winter; a renaissance of color, flowering buds, the fresh morning dew for spring; and the warmth and freedom of the summer shore. When you think of fruit, do you think only of apples and oranges? Or do you have rich associations of color, texture, taste, size, weight, shape, and other such qualities? The period of early childhood is the ideal time for such rich associations as these to develop through concrete experience, as we will see in subsequent chapters. Early education must emphasize and nurture the young child's ability to explore, which is innate and cannot be taught or artificially augmented. The child herself must be the ultimate concept builder. *Concept learning is potentially the most important learning that she will participate in during the course of her entire lifetime.* All the parent and teacher can really do is be around when the child needs resources and assistance, and give her love and support. The child will do the rest, as long as there are adequate resources available for her to explore and discover. Early sensory learning is certainly creative discovery.

In Part 2 of this text, you will find descriptions of materials and activities which have been found to be useful in enriching the young child's environment and assuring a maximization of opportunities for growth and development. Sensory development should begin at a very early age and develop naturally. The child is desperately longing for sensory experience and conceptual meaning. It is important to remember, at all times, *that the best experiences in early childhood are the unstructured ones that allow the child to utilize her natural gifts of exploration.*[9] Lowenfeld has found the coloring book to be potentially a most destructive invention, for it limits the child to coloring between predetermined lines.[10] Commercially produced toys can also be extremely limiting, if their use is completely predetermined and programmed by the manufacturer. The child should be left as free as possible to develop her own materials, uses, functions, and aesthetics. Children need to develop, create, and validate their own personal meanings, and it is through this process that they develop true intelligence and their own personal identity.

5

Learning and Concept Formation

The theory of stages of development, as explained by Piaget and other developmental psychologists, is an important part of the story of early learning, but it is not the whole story.[1] Much early learning certainly derives from the natural processes of the interaction between the young child and his environment, through the mechanisms of adaptation, assimilation, and accommodation.[2] However, there are also other learning mechanisms that have a significant bearing upon early child development and subsequent learning throughout life. These other processes are usually described under the heading, theories of learning.[3] Where stages of development explain the natural development of the child and his levels of readiness, learning theories more readily describe the *process of education.* For the parent and teacher, a thorough knowledge of both developmental theory and learning theory is vitally important for successful intervention in the process of human development and particularly in the enrichment of early learning.

Learning Theories

Conditioned Learning

The most fundamental process of learning is called *association,* which is the process by which a child begins to learn adaptive responses to his environment. Events that occur together in time and in space become identified with each other.[4] This happens either when two stimuli occur together or when a stimulus and a response are related to one another. An infant's crying usually stimulates the attention of the mother; the association of the stimulus (crying) and the response (mother's attention) is *reinforced* by the pleasure that is forthcoming from the attention. This behavior link between stimulus and response will likely continue, as long as a pleasurable response is the result of the infant's crying. The stimulus and the response link that develops is referred to as *conditioned learning*. The response in such a behavioral situation is referred to as a *positive reinforcer* because it tends to maintain, or increase, the strength of the infant's behavior. The infant begins to know that each time he cries, the result will be a pleasurable sensation. This will be the case even before the infant is fully aware of the nature of the mother as primary caretaker.

The most famous experiments in conditioned learning through association occurred in the laboratory of Ivan Pavlov, the great Russian psychologist, during the 1920s.[5] Pavlov is particulary well-known for his work with dogs as subjects. Pavlov would attach a measurement device to his canine subjects in order to measure their rate of salivation when presented with food. During the early stages of his experiments, Pavlov would ring a bell and then feed his dogs. Through the process of association, one stimulus (the bell) was linked to another stimulus (the food), and then the dogs began to expect the food to follow the bell on all occasions. This bond between the bell and the food was *positively reinforced* by the pleasure the dogs obtained from eating the food. After a while, Pavlov deceived his subjects by ringing the bell but not presenting the food. He was able to measure the dogs' expectancy for the food by his salivation measurement device. Indeed, the dogs continued to salivate every time the bell was rung, even though the food was not forthcoming. However, the link between the bell and the food gradually diminished since it was not being reinforced, and eventually the association totally disappeared.[6]

Experiments like Pavlov's have continued unabated since these pioneering studies, and the importance of conditioned learning is generally accepted by psychologists and educators, particularly in early learning. At the extreme, some psychologists hold that almost all learning can be conditioned and that association learning is the most fundamental unit of human learning.[7] From simple observation of early infant behavior, it is hard to deny that a great deal of association learning is occurring. The young infant rarely initiates behavior and tends to depend upon external stimulation to which he reacts. Infant responses tend to be reinforced in any number of ways, although most frequently through feelings of pleasure and security, even if these feelings are not readily observable. Early infant learning is generally considered to be *incidental learning,* because it occurs largely through chance associations rather than specific instruction or intent. The more a response is reinforced, intentionally or incidentally, the greater will be the *response strength* and the probability of the response occurring again. If the infant is constantly reinforced for crying, for example, the behavior will become consistent and reliable.[8]

Although human learning appears to be much more complex than association as learning theorists would have us believe, there is little doubt about the value of such theory. It has largely been through research in simple learning that we have acquired the wealth of psychological knowledge that we currently possess. The realization of the similarities between animal learning and basic human learning has permitted psychologists to refine their knowledge by experimenting with animals, aware that their findings are largely valid for many aspects of human learning as well. If you explore the extensive literature on learning, you will find that much of it is a result of experiments with animals. However, in viewing this type of research, be acutely aware of the limitations of these animal studies.[9]

Trial-and-Error Learning

Once the young child becomes able to manipulate the elements of his environment to some extent, new developments in learning begin to occur. This is the notion of *trial-and-error learning.* It is similar to simple association learning in that a stimulus and a response connection occurs and is reinforced. In trial-and-error learning the child is becoming a more active participant in the learning process. Through this type of learning, the young child learns most of his early lessons. He tries to do something, and he continues to try until he succeeds. This success reinforces the connection between the stimulus and the response (which has been refined through the trial-and-error process). The young child engages in this type of active learning adventure every day, sometimes hundreds of times each day.[10]

An interesting example of trial-and-error learning is the manner in which a young child learns to grasp an object. It is a gradual process of trying different grasping methods until partial, and then complete, success is achieved. At first the child might try to grasp the object in the palm of his tiny hand. Failing at that impossible strategy, he might try to do it with a combination of fingers. The trial-and-error learning process can be a rewarding one, but it can also be occasionally frustrating. It is fascinating to watch children attempting a task such as grasping; their concentration is remarkable. Eventually, though, both partial and complete success causes a strong bond to form between the stimulus (the object) and the response (the proper grasping procedure); this learning will become a significant part of the child's perceptual-motor skill repertoire. Pure trial-and-error learning is highly individualistic, and the solution will depend upon the fortuitous combination of circumstances, which we usually refer to as *luck*. The young child does not really have any strategy for solving the problem or any systematic way of approaching it. He will probably try every possible combination of motor responses that he is capable of mastering until either he loses interest or achieves some measure of success.[11]

Successive Approximation Learning

Another method of approaching the problem of early association learning is called the *successive approximation method*. It is through successive approximations of the correct response that the child is gradually *led* to the correct solution. This is often recommended, especially when the child appears frustrated with trial-and-error experiences. This learning method includes another person in the learning process, someone to gradually guide the learner to the correct solution such as, in the example above, the proper grasping procedure. In the successive approximation method, the learner is reinforced for behaviors which are "on the right track." This dispels the possibility of the frustration that can result from the "all-or-nothing" approach which is built into trial-and-error learning. When the child seems to be developing the proper grasp, even though he might not be having much practical success, he is praised, or reinforced in some other way, to indicate to him that he is on the way to eventual solution of the problem at hand. This method will undoubtedly reduce the time it takes for the child to learn a skill, and it will also virtually eliminate the chance of frustration. However, there is also the possibility that this instructional method will reduce the feeling of success and competence that results from independent exploration and problem solving. Thus, if the parent or teacher is going to become active in the learning process, it is recommended that this intervention be as unobtrusive as possible, especially for simple learnings. The adult can always be in the background to make sure that the child does not become frustrated. Successive approximation methods should be used for tasks which are difficult enough to require adult assistance. Children who are not allowed sufficient trial-and-error experience may develop a lack of self-reliance and feel less of a sense of overall competence.

When using the successive approximation method, or some variation of it, it is important to understand the notion of schedules of reinforcement.[12] Schedules of reinforcement relate to the frequency with which correct or nearly correct responses are reinforced. If reinforcement occurs after every appropriate response, the child may become overly dependent upon it. This may make him less likely to respond properly when reinforcement is not forthcoming. Furthermore, a "100 percent reinforcement schedule", as it is called, has been shown to cause a more rapid deterioration of the response (or forgetting). It is important that young learners do not become too dependent upon reinforcement for their satisfactions, since success in obtaining new skills should be satisfying in itself.[13] Learning is a very exciting process which can be made less so through excessive external reinforcement. As a result of these considerations, "partial reinforcement schedules" have been found to be much more satisfactory in both successive approximation learning and other association learning experiences. This explains why Pavlov's dogs lost their salivation response so rapidly following the termination of reinforcement.

B. F. Skinner has been the most famous proponent of successive approximation learning. He and his followers believe that you can teach anybody to do anything through these fundamental conditioning methods.[14] This may be an exaggeration, but there is little doubt as to the potency of these techniques. Currently, successive approximation methods are being successfully used to train the mentally retarded, to teach people simple skills, and to help people learn to do things that they were previously frightened of doing. For example, children who were frightened of animals have been conditioned, through successive approximation, to be less frightened of them. Animals are brought gradually closer to these children and the children are encouraged and reinforced along the way. Eventually, the child comes in direct contact with the animal and learns that there is really nothing to be frightened of. The success of these methods has been startling. Another use of a similar technique is through the use of programmed textbooks and teaching machines.[15] In such learning experiences, students are gradually led through difficult subject matter in small, easily digestible steps. The idea of these texts is to minimize error and to reinforce the student for making the correct response along the way. These texts have proven to be very successful, especially for slow learners, particularly when supplemented with other instructional experiences.

Knowledge of this type of instruction can be valuable for the parent or teacher when faced with a difficult or unpleasant learning situation. Not every child is inherently motivated to learn every skill.[16] Sometimes gentle persuasion and successive approximation techniques should and must be used. However, it is recommended that the adult be careful that the child is not being deprived of a valuable *independent* learning experience. It really is a case of having to assess the nature of the learning task with respect to the abilities of the learner. Is the task difficult or unpleasant? Is the learner capable of achieving the goal on his own? Does he have the prerequisite abilities? The best way to decide these questions is through common sense and careful observation of the individual child. It is virtually impossible to derive reliable generalizations concerning the readiness of children to undertake a specific skill independently at a certain level of development or chronological age.[17] Perhaps the best piece of advice is for you to allow the child to start the task on his own and see what happens. If it appears too difficult or if success is still too remote, simply change your instructional strategy with no harm done.

The best way to assure successful learning is through the selection of appropriate learning tasks for the child, tasks that are neither too easy nor too difficult. If the tasks are too easy, the child will not feel a sense of challenge or as much pride in accomplishment. If the task is too difficult, the child may be frustrated, and the experience of learning may be needlessly painful. However, if we have learned anything from Piagetian theory, it is that the child must ultimately be in charge of his own learning and that learning tasks may be initially difficult, yet this difficulty may lead to important strides in terms of environmental adaptation.[18]

There is another factor involved in the learning process—punishment. Punishment tends to decrease the probability of the occurrence of a certain response, and it certainly has its place in learning. However, evidence indicates that positive reinforcement is far more effective than punishment in facilitating learning.[19] The problem with punishment is that, when used, a child's first learning experiences can become associated with unpleasant feelings. In addition, it only tells the child what an incorrect response is, but not what the correct response is. The feeling of competence that is so important for the young child will develop through success and positive feelings.

One fascinating line of research is the notion of "learned helplessness."[20] It has recently been found that consistent failure or continual punishment can become habit-forming. Failure and punishment can eventually lead a child into feeling that he is incompetent, and he frequently stops trying. The lesson is apparent; early learning experiences can lead to feelings of success and competence or to feelings of failure and incompetence. It is important that learning experiences be structured in such a way as to maximize the probability of the former and minimize the probability of the latter.

It is interesting to note that many early childhood educational materials are developed in such a way that the child will be more likely to have positive experiences with them. The instructional materials developed by Montessori in her early childhood training programs are engineered in such a manner that the materials are self-correcting.[21] For example, there are cylinders of different sizes that can be fitted into appropriate holes. Montessori has arranged the activity so that there is only one way that all the cylinders can fit into the holes. Thus, the child cannot make an error; the idea being the elimination of failure. This is the very same objective espoused by Skinner's programmed instruction materials. It is also a very effective philosophy that we should all consider. In a very real sense, success breeds success.

Generalization

Once a child has learned basic associations, he still has a great deal of learning to accomplish. Associative learning is of little value unless the skills so learned can generalize to other situations and learning tasks. *Generalization,* or transfer, is the process through which a person learns to react to similar stimuli or situations as if they were the same. Actually, generalization is not always a learned process. The very young infant tends to view a great many objects and people as fundamentally the same. His reaction to all people is the same until he is able to recognize the "distinctive features" of each individual. Many objects which are similar in shape may well appear to be the same object until the child has had more experience with a variety of objects and with his world in general. When certain stimuli (such as objects or people) are viewed as being essentially the same, this is called *stimulus generalization.* Certainly all of us must have had numerous personal experiences with this type of generalization, by mistaking one person for another or one house for another.

There is another type of generalization that is far more important from a learning theory point-of-view—*response generalization.* This type of generalization occurs when we tend to respond to different stimulus situations as if they were the same. For example, when we see a police officer, we tend to behave in a certain way, even though we are certainly aware that each police officer is a unique individual. Response generalization is often referred to as *transfer of training* in education. This means that what we learn in one area can be transferred, or generalized, to another area. This makes it possible for us to be economical in our learning. Actually, generalization is a key factor in concept learning, as we will soon see. Jerome Bruner has referred to concept learning as the ability to "go beyond the information given."[22] In a very real sense, this is what learned generalization or transfer means. It allows us to respond to our world in terms of perceived similarities and respond to these similar things as if they were equal.

Discrimination

However, as important as generalization is in human learning, there are limits to its usefulness. Generalization can cause us to oversimplify our world. If we begin to see everything as similar and react in a similar fashion to all these things, then life will become a constant confusion. The learning process that helps us deal with generalization in a realistic manner is called *discrimination*. Discrimination helps us recognize the dissimilarities in our physical world and tends to limit generalization. For example, as we see the similarities among various classes of people, we also learn to see the attributes of these people that make them different. For example, we learn to distinguish different kinds of fruit from the generalized category *fruit*. So we can see that generalization and discrimination are complementary mental processes. The effects of generalization *ad infinitum* would be horrendous indeed!

Gradually, the infant learns that there are special members of the generalized class *adults*—the mother and the father. These individuals give the child special treatment. The process of generalization is much easier than the process of discrimination, and, of course, the process of association is the most basic of all. However, these three complementary processes occur rather naturally for all of us. Whether or not we are specifically instructed in associations, generalizations, and discriminations, we will probably learn this lesson adequately. However, those who have more experience, who practice their newly acquired skills, will probably develop more refined capabilities faster. Early experience will most probably positively affect future learning experiences.[23]

Higher-Level Learning

When we consider the interaction, or overlap, among association, generalization, and discrimination, we are discussing what most psychologists and educators refer to as "higher-level learning." This is the beginning of mature learning in which experiences need not be treated individually, and they can be classified into experiential categories, or concepts. Consider the "grasping response" example again. The child first learns to grasp an object through a prolonged period of trial-and-error activity. Eventually, the child becomes able to grasp the object through the successful association of grasping techniques and the coordination of these skills into a correct grasping response. This skill becomes particularly useful when the child learns to generalize it to other similar objects. The child will eventually fail when he tries to use this same grasping response with vastly different objects. He must learn that he should use a different grasping technique for a square object than he uses for a round object, and vice versa. This is learned through the process of discrimination and is perhaps the most painstaking process in early learning.

The very young child often has great difficulty in drawing a tree that is readily distinguishable from a flower. The child is able to associate a pictorial representation of a tree with the real-life object and a drawing of a flower with the real flower. He is able to generalize the similar characteristics of "things that grow from the ground." However, he is not yet ready to distinguish the unique characteristics of each and draw them as such. The idea of size difference is a difficult one to learn, as are the more subtle distinctive characteristics of trees and flowers. Such learning takes time and experience with different examples in the environment. Some children need more time than others to learn to discriminate effectively, but such learning is generally a function of the amount of experience the children have with common things in the environment.[24]

The learning process can be viewed as a "hierarchy of experience." First, a vast number of basic associations are formed. Then, these associations are generalized to other objects, ideas, and situations. Finally, these "generalized associations" are made more practically useful through the process of discrimination; the learned skills become appropriate to the demands of the real world. This process through which experience is refined into learning which is relevant to the demands of the real world is illustrated in Figure 1.

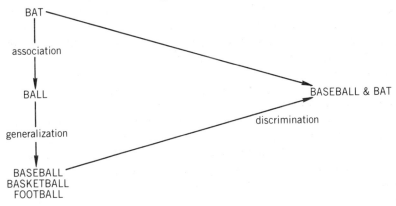

Figure 1

Example of the complementary processes of association, generalization, and discrimination in concept learning

Once an appropriate learning strategy is formed, it can be used in many different situations with ease and facility. This is the nature of "concept learning." Through the complementary learning processes described above, the young child learns "patterns" of experience and behavior. He learns to free himself of the constraints of the specific situation; he frees himself from having to learn everything in a trial-and-error manner every time he is exposed to something new. After a while, the grasping response becomes a grasping concept, as the basic associations formed acquire appropriate generalizations and discriminations. Thus, the child learns to go beyond the information given and is able to develop his own learning and experiential strategies. This is the first major step a child takes toward achieving true competence, as well as a measure of autonomy and independence.

There is still more to the story of human learning. Most psychologists and educators believe that there is another element that enters into the process of learning. This highest level of human intellectual activity is generally referred to as *thinking*.[25] On the basis of previous learning, we can generate new information. Thinking is the process, the abstract process (sometimes called a "mediating process"), through which we are able to derive new categories of experience from old ones. For instance, the child first has to try out different objects to discover whether they are similar or different from ones he has experienced previously, but gradually he learns to do this internally. We learn to recognize similar and distinguishing characteristics, and we develop behavioral strategies for dealing with these perceived characteristics. This is the level of mental activity that most instruction aims at facilitating. This is the level of autonomous learning, which is uniquely human. Humans are not like Pavlov's dogs, at least not for long! From the time that we develop functional categories of experience, we tend to interpret future learning with these categories; indeed, they are the ultimate tools of learning. It is through the interaction of experience and concepts that our thought processes tend to mature.[26] Through conceptual learning, everyday experience becomes a constant process of learning. The more examples of the color green that we experience, the richer that concept becomes. The more objects that the young child has the opportunity to grasp, the richer his grasping concept becomes, and the more able he is to manipulate his environment. Conceptual learning is a continual process of growth, a process by which learning becomes refined through subsequent learning. This process is illustrated in Figure 2.

Our concepts are continually updated and refined. The more chances we have to enrich our existing categories and to form new ones, the better able we become to deal with our environment. Thus, we can see the central importance of concept formation in human learning. It is one of the most remarkable natural phenomena that human beings are able to organize their experiences in this way.

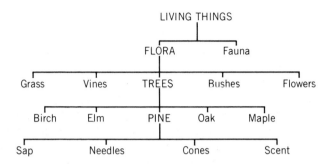

Figure 2

Example of how refinement of conceptual categories occurs through experience with our physical world

Early concept learning, as discussed previously, is usually concerned with defining categories in terms of a single attribute. An example of this is "round things." With additional experience, such simple categories become further defined by other attributes. An example of this might be "round, green things" or "round, red things." The process of conceptual refinement continues until we have defined our concepts to the point at which they are as functional as possible. To some, a tree might be a "large green growth," while to others it may be a "living plant that is usually tall, with a wooden trunk articulated with branches covered with leaves."

In summary, we have seen that concept learning is the result of the interaction of three complementary learning processes: association, generalization, and discrimination. *Association* helps the learner establish bonds between stimuli, and between stimuli and responses. This is the most basic type of learning. *Generalization* is the process by which the learner is able to extend his learning through using it in new situations. However, generalization needs limits; this is the role of *discrimination.* For most everything in our world, there are similarities and differences. Successful learning depends upon this recognition and subsequent utilization. It is through these learning processes that human activity rises to a higher level, the level of thought. Concept learning makes it possible to "go beyond the information given" and economize on future learning. It is through the use of conceptual categories, and their constant refinement, that we can depend upon and utilize previous experience to become efficient learners. In this way, learning becomes both *cumulative* and *hierarchical,* with all subsequent learning depending upon previous learning.[27] In the light of this evidence, it becomes apparent how vitally important it is to lay a firm and rich foundation for future conceptual learning and experience. The growth of rich categories in children is a major developmental task. It will soon become apparent how the young child begins groping for regularity and for the knowledge that comes through organized experience.

The key word in early childhood instruction is *organization.* The environment of the young child should not be chaotic; it should be representative of the way in which you hope the child will develop his intellectual abilities. The importance of quantity of experience is stressed in this book, but the need for some organization of that experience is assumed. The world of the young child is totally new, and it can be overpowering, unless care is taken to present new experiences in an orderly fashion.

6

The Stages of Concept Formation

Adults tend to take concept formation for granted, for we rarely remember the long and arduous process through which we developed our own functional concepts in early childhood. For the young child, this process is a difficult but exciting experience, drawing together increasing experiential evidence and grouping it into categories in order to assure efficient interaction with the environment. Concepts do not just pop up; they develop gradually and naturally with appropriate experience, maturation, and intellectual growth. There is no reason to rush this process, or any other developmental process. Adults should lay the foundation and supply the raw materials of experience; the young child will do the rest. However, it is valuable to understand the mechanisms by which concepts develop and form. In this chapter, two parallel theories of concept formation will be described. They possess many similarities and tend to augment and complement each other. One theory has been presented by the Russian psychologist L. S. Vygotsky;[1] the other theory has been developed by Jean Piaget, through his extensive work with his collaborator Barbel Inhelder.[2] The stages of the two theories are compared below:

Vygotsky's Theory	Piaget's Theory
1. heaps	1. graphic collections
2. associative complexes	a. collective alignments
3. collections	b. collective objects
4. chain complexes	c. complex objects
5. diffuse complexes	2. nongraphic collections
6. pseudo-concepts	3. concepts
7. concepts	

Two Theories of Concept Formation

General Aspects

These two theories are really quite similar to each other in most substantive aspects.[3] Before going on to a specific explanation of each, we will briefly explore some of the more general aspects of early concept formation. Both theorists believe that there are stages in the development process that precede the formation of mature concepts; that is, there are prerequisites for mature concept formation, the foundation upon which optimal concepts are built. According to both of these views, and others, concepts develop from very unassuming beginnings. The major developmental task is the decentering of the child's impressions of the world from purely perceptual characteristics to higher-level, more abstract, characteristics.[4] At first, the young child is totally bound by what her senses tell her. She is also bound by what she has seen last. In other words, when categorizing objects, the very young child tends to group things according to personal preference or some characteristic of the last object encountered, rather than by some grand intellectual design.[5] For example, before the child is ready for more mature forms of conceptualization, she may be easily distracted by irrelevant characteristics of the items she is grouping. If asked to group items according to color, she may become distracted by size and then go on to group the items according to that criterion. According to both Vygotsky and Piaget, unless there is a "grand design," and the child is aware of precisely what she is doing, these precursors to true concept formation are not yet the real thing. Vygotsky's reference to *complexes* and Piaget's reference to *collections* are really part of the same notion. The stage names and their sequence vary slightly, but the point that both are explaining is practically identical: that very young children are not ready for higher levels of concept learning. It is not just a matter of lack of training; it is much more importantly a matter of lack of readiness. There is no need to rush this readiness; it will come naturally. In the meantime, the most appropriate thing to do is to give the young child practice and experience at those stages of conceptual growth for which she is ready.[6]

Both theorists agree that young children enjoy grouping things, but at first these groupings are totally individualistic and egocentric.[7] They begin grouping according to immediate desires, for reasons of aesthetic preference perhaps, but not as a result of a deep understanding of the relationships between things and their characteristics. Vygotsky describes the first stage of the process as the formation of *heaps,* piles of things grouped together for no substantial reason. Sometimes there is the appearance of design; yet, more often than not, this appearance is highly deceptive, the result of chance. Piaget views the first stage of conceptual development as being *graphic collections,* items that are not related to each other in a *conceptual* way but are put together because the result is perceptually pleasing to the child. For instance, the child will put objects in a line or some other geometrical shape because of the total effect, not because the items generically belong together. Although it is difficult to see the relationship between these early steps and mature concept formation, both Vygotsky and Piaget view them as just that: important steps on the way to more mature intellectual functioning.

The very young child, for example a two year old, is not quite ready to put different shapes together into coherent groups with one shape to a group, e.g., circles in one group, triangles in another, and squares in a third. More likely, the child will work with these shapes in ways apparently unrelated to their fundamental attributes. The development of the ability to *abstract* characteristics from the items, like *roundness, triangularness,* and *squareness,* is still not adequately developed, nor should it be. There are yet important developmental tasks for the child to accomplish. Each will come in its proper time and sequence. Let us look a little more closely at these two models of concept development.

Vygotsky's Theory

Vygotsky presents his model in his book *Thought and Language,* in which he has hypothesized the development of early grouping strategies called *complexes,* distinguishing them from the end products of the concept formation process.[8] These early complexes are formed mostly through the process of *association,* discussed earlier. Experiences are grouped because of preference, location together in space, similarity of appearance, or other such reasons.[9]

It is quite a natural thing for young children to group objects into heaps of things, often for no substantial reason. Gradually, the child begins to understand the relationships between objects and their similarities. Through this process, these basic groupings begin to have more meaning. Meaning is the content of concepts. The more experience young children have with the things in their environment, the more meaningful their concepts become.

Complex development begins with the unification of scattered sensory impressions.[10] The young child, in the first year of life, is constantly bombarded with visual information, and it is important that she develop some way of associating and interpreting these impressions for later use. Little is known of these early groupings of sensory impressions because there is really no way of measuring them. Perhaps the most basic type of grouping is the way we form integrated visual impressions from isolated sensory data. Through perceptual cues, such as color, form, shape, light intensity, and distinctive details, humans are able to develop an integrated picture of the visual world. This is probably the earliest type of concept the child develops. In a real sense, it is an interplay of association and discrimination, on a purely perceptual level. Initially the young child must piece together sensory impressions from the rich environment, associate essential elements, and discriminate them from irrelevant elements. This is the basic idea behind the ability to distinguish between figure and background, perhaps the foremost principle of human perception.

As soon as the infant has mastered the ability to focus on objects within her field of vision, she is able to explore objects and identify them by their distinguishing characteristics. Every exploratory act the young child engages in includes some form of categorizing. A child learns to classify people according to their appearances and their actions. She is able to associate certain features and behaviors with her parents, and this association is usually very pleasurable (and, thus, is reinforced). When the parent approaches, the child reacts with a smile. These basic associations are not of great importance in themselves but add up to form an experiential base for future concept formation. It is valuable to view all association learning as the "raw material of concepts." Although undifferentiated and vague, these early associations represent rich experience. Later the child will learn to further group these early associations, distinguish relevant from irrelevant characteristics, and learn to make finer and finer discriminations.

The *external concepts* in a young child's life cannot be overemphasized.[11] The young child's environment is usually very carefully ordered by parents and teachers and is initially quite limited. The newborn child is unable to explore by herself; her environment must be brought to her. The more richness the child experiences early, the more variety of experience she will be motivated to seek when able to explore actively on her own. The adult has a huge responsibility in terms of forming external concepts and environmental planning. Much as the urban planner is responsible for planning the efficiency of urban life, the parent or teacher is responsible for planning an environment for the child which will maximize her contact with novel and exciting stimuli.

When the child has mastered heaps, she is ready to move on to a more sophisticated type of complex development, associative complexes. *Associative complexes* are groups formed consistently on the basis of a common trait, similarity, proximity, or some other objective criterion.

One object usually serves as the nucleus for such grouping, and other objects are added because of their similarity or proximity to that object. One type of similarity utilized consistently is objective *consistency* which makes associative complexes fundamentally different from heaps.

Next, the child develops the ability to form collections. *Collections* are contrasting or complementary groups. Cups and saucers; spoons, knives and forks; suits of clothes; and dogs and cats are examples of these complexes. Through the formation of such collections, the child learns to group things that complement each other, on the basis of past experience and functional relationships.

Following collections, the child learns to form chain complexes. *Chain complexes* are groupings based on changing associations. For instance, a child may begin grouping on the basis of shape, then continue grouping on the basis of color, and so forth. The value of this type of grouping is that it provides the child with an increased flexibility of association. This is primarily the realization that conceptual groupings can be based on a very large number of attributes. For instance, a *red circle* can be categorized as part of the concept *red things* or the concept *circular things.* A *postman* is a *person,* a *man dressed in blue,* a *civil servant,* and any number of other things. It takes considerable time and effort for the child to realize the great multiplicity of possible associations that eventually lead to more mature forms of concept grouping.

The next type of complex grouping is called diffuse complexes. These carry on where chain complexes leave off. In this stage, there is not so much a change in grouping strategy as much as a refinement of this ability. Diffuse complexes are marked by an increased flexibility of association. They utilize intermediate associations.[12] For instance, a child who is categorizing triangles might add a square to her group, "because the square looks like two triangles, one right-side-up, the other up-side-down." Indeed, the child is correct; however, her response is a distraction from the task at hand. Diffuse complexes can show great creativity, and these responses should be encouraged. They show that the child is beginning to participate in more mature thought processes and is becoming less tied to immediate perception only. She is now truly *thinking,* thinking about attributes of things and relating them to each other. The possibilities for grouping in this way are virtually unlimited, and it is a revelation to witness the creative combinations that can result.

From diffuse complexes, the child soon moves on to pseudo-concepts, in which she is forming conceptual groupings but frequently is not quite sure of the precise nature of the task. The child in the example above may indeed group all the proper shapes together; however, she is probably not yet able to specify the "rule" for grouping. The result is the same as in true concept formation, but the "rule" (the reason) for grouping has not been wholly grasped. However, at this point, the child is very close to true concept formation, and well on the way to developing mature intellectual processes.

Concept formation then is the result of the foregoing process of stages and constant consolidation of each development. The result is a natural development of a sense of "classes" of things and an awareness that everything in the world has properties, attributes, and characteristics which are shared by other things, even if they do not look exactly alike. A large, red square is a square as much as a small, yellow square. A small ranch house is just as much a house for those who live in it as is a huge, fifty-room mansion for the occupants of that dwelling. The process of moving away from a dependency on perception toward the ability to "abstract" the properties of things is a long and painstaking process, but it is an exciting one. The insights of Vygotsky's model help us understand the steps from concrete to abstract thinking.

Piaget's Theory

Piaget's model is quite similar and equally as useful. According to his view, there are three major stages: graphic collections, nongraphic collections, and, finally, concepts.

As previously mentioned, graphic collections are groupings which are formed without concern for the attributes of the items at hand. They are formed for individual and perceptual reasons, for pleasure, for immediate interest, and for artistic appeal. They are not formed because the child has mastered the nature of the similarities and differences among the items. It may very well be that the child will exhibit some ability to put a few similar items together, but this response will not be consistent or enduring.

The stage of *graphic collections* is seen by Piaget to be divided into three basic substages. The first substage is *collective alignments,* in which the child begins to put items together in a line. The child may have the beginning of an awareness of basic similarities, but this is still very primitive. As Piaget explains, although there may be similarities between successive elements, there is no prior design involved, no anticipation that the result will be a group of items that is "alike."[13] These alignments are very similar to Vygotsky's notion of associative complexes. *Collective objects* form the next substage of graphic collections, in which the child produces a more complex collection of items in more than one dimension.

The child is beginning to react more consistently to item similarities, but still these similarities and successive groupings are secondary to the overall graphic collection. The next substage is *complex objects,* in which the child compiles more coherent and meaningful collections, but the overall collection is still more important than the internal similarities among items. In all these examples, the child may intend to group items according to the criterion of similarity but loses sight of that original purpose and becomes interested primarily in the perceptual and aesthetic characteristics of the graphic creation.

It must be made clear that these stages in concept development are normal developmental steps. When young children are engaged in creating graphic collections, they are not ready for more mature grouping. However, the attempt is still important in itself, and the child should be given ample opportunity to engage in this type of grouping activity. Ultimately, successful concept grouping will be achieved; in the meantime, the process is much more important than the product. In Piaget's view, of most importance, is not that children cannot group items according to similarities, but that they often get distracted by the graphic nature of the task along the way. Any true conceptual grouping must, according to Piaget, be intentional.[14] There is no clear transition from graphic collections to nongraphic collections. These stages tend to overlap, just like most developmental trends in early childhood. In fact, the primitive basis for nongraphic collections seems to co-exist with graphic collections from the very beginning. The transition is one of grouping according to similarity *by chance* to doing it *intentionally.* Unfortunately, the difference is not easy to see.

Piaget views the transition from graphic collections to nongraphic collections as usually occurring sometime during the fourth year. This is the point at which the child is beginning to show considerable mental flexibility. She starts grouping items according to one characteristic and continues this process with little distraction. A child this age begins to sort geometrical shapes into appropriate piles. Where the younger child might become distracted by the resulting shapes of the collection, the older child is more concerned with the grouping task at hand and seeing it through to completion. Early in the graphic collection stage, there are still inconsistencies and ambiguities. At first, the child may not be able to group all items and may leave some items ungrouped. She also might be unable to group items consistently on the basis of a single criterion, by color for instance. Eventually, she is able to group items on the basis of continually changing criteria; for example, first grouping into piles of like shapes, then dividing these into groups of similar colors.[15] The emphasis here is obviously on the categorizing itself, and gradually the child develops more and more a sense of intention and purpose. This is the development that Piaget feels is so vital to more mature forms of intellectual activity.

Nongraphic collections differ from true concepts in degree rather than in kind. The difference is really in the ability of the child to change criteria at will and to be able to "anticipate" the overall design of the task from the beginning.[16] Piaget's idea of true concepts is really one of elevating the mental process from trial-and-error to the mental premeditation of the final outcome. The characteristic *roundness* becomes an abstract feature which transcends the individual appearance of items. Items are round if they possess that abstract property, no matter what color or size they might be. In true concept formation, there is no need to compare items perceptually. At this new level of intellectual attainment, the differences and similarities are grasped at a higher level, at the level of *abstraction*.[17]

The transition from more primitive forms of grouping is a long and trying process for the child. It must be accomplished in small and measured steps. However, this gradual transition from perceptually based thought to abstract thought may well be the most important developmental process in early childhood.[18] Since all learning is hierarchical, care must be taken to firmly establish and consolidate the previous steps. It is hoped that this chapter and the discussion of two important theories of conceptual development will provide you with some guidance as to what to expect from the child as her intellectual processes mature. It will also give you a foundation of knowledge from which you can better appreciate the tremendous intellectual gains that are continually occurring.

7

Early Conceptual Experiences

Basic concept formation is the most appropriate learning of early childhood. The most elementary groupings of experience are developed as the child combines the diverse sensory information that constantly bombards him: the light stimulating the nerve cells of the retina of the eye, the sound waves entering the ear, the tactile impressions of touch, and the taste buds reacting to the sweetness and sourness of foods.[1] The child slowly begins to associate various sensations with objects. A smile for mother and father, a grasp at a familiar object, a reaction to a familiar sound, and pleasure after a sweet taste. It does not take long before the child is able to construct basic *associations,* the raw material for subsequent concepts. It is important that we do not underrate these early accomplishments. If we realize the importance of these early associations, we can expand on them and build more sophisticated associations and discriminations.

As Piaget has explained, the intellectual development of the child is primarily the result of his own action alone.[2] Adults can present varied and organized stimulation, but it is up to the child himself to act upon these stimuli and use them. The child is born with this desire and ability. His constant activity is a very real occurrence. Whether the child is actively grasping or quietly observing, tremendous intellectual changes are occurring, and new learnings are being assimilated. Few adults have the time to systematically observe children as carefully as Piaget did, but it would certainly be an instructive experience to try from time to time. Piaget recorded almost every new response and experience of his children and enriched their environments by constantly presenting them with novel stimuli and situations.[3] Reading his books is difficult, but his careful and meticulous descriptions of his children's achievements interspersed in the text make wonderful and rewarding reading.

Stimulation Must Be Presented to the Infant

It would be a worthwhile experience for you to try to put yourself in the position of the very young child for a few moments and consider the magnitude of the things he has to learn as he tries to fit the world to himself and fit himself to the world. Even focusing his attention on specific objects in his environment is an achievement of monumental proportions. At first, the newborn's vision is relatively uncoordinated; he has no idea what to fixate his attention upon. The child's first clear visual image is a parent, a face in focus in the vastness of an out-of-focus world. It is some time before the child is able to visually explore even his nursery, and that is why it is so urgent that the young infant's visual environment be brought to him. If we are to heed the lessons of developmental psychologists, including Piaget, it is up to the parent to construct a variety of experiences for the infant and place them within the infant's field of vision. Bright colors, simple shapes, and lively mobiles are highly recommended for stimulating the infant's visual exploration, for training his attention, and encouraging the construction of a store of sensory information. Although the infant does not *understand* the colors and shapes that are presented to him at this point, this information will be remembered. It is never too early to begin this stimulation, for the newborn child is truly a finely tuned learning machine; he will devour new information and stimulation when it is brought to him.[4] Later, when this information becomes functional for recognition purposes, evidence indicates that learning will be easier and concepts will be richer. The child without this early stimulation will probably not develop as rapidly or as completely as the child with it.[5]

The young child is inherently curious. He will explore as soon as he is able to do so. It is tremendously important that this curiosity not be stifled by an unsatisfying environment. A bare, white nursery is not a very stimulating environment. The child who is subject to early sensory deprivation is beginning his life with a very severe handicap.[6] Curiosity seems to breed curiosity, and it is evident from research that *the more the child sees, the more he wants to see;* the more he does, the more he wants to do; the greater the variety of objects that become familiar to him, the more rapid his intellectual growth will develop.

During the sensorimotor period, the child sees everything revolving around himself. He has little realization of a world separate from himself.[7] The first concept he has to learn is *object permanence,* for through it the basic knowledge of a world, separate from self, emerges. Although this early model of the world changes and matures with subsequent learnings, there is ample evidence to indicate that many aspects of this model remain. The attention of the parent, the emphasis upon early stimulation, the encouragement of exploration, the supportive smile, the lack of punishment, the attractiveness of the environment, the opportunities to assimilate new information, and the intellectual exercise of accommodation to environmental demands are aspects of the young child's world that remain as the primary memories of early childhood.

Early experiences should be active, sensory, and manipulative.[8] The parent and teacher should present the child with stimuli which will provide him with a variety of sensory and manipulative experiences. It is through such experiences, as will be described in later chapters, and sensory stimulation that the child develops his perceptual abilities, and, through progressively finer manipulation, the child develops his motor coordination and physical ability. *Perception* and *motor coordination* are the foundation for intellectual growth, for it is through the process of perception that we "take in" our world and through motor coordination that we act upon it.[9]

Variety Important

Early experience should deal with a great variety of things—colorful things; graspable things; things of different shapes, sizes, and textures; heavy things; light things; child-size things; movable things; soft things; hard things. The world of variety and change must be brought to the child in quantity. Very young children cannot say, "I'm bored." or "Give me more stimulation." The adult must anticipate the child's needs, and the research on early childhood education is very clear on this point: very young children need constant stimulation in order to exercise, train, and expand their new perceptual abilities.[10] Eyesight will develop without extraordinary stimulation, but it may not become as sensitive as possible. The ears of the child will become acute auditory instruments with practice; body muscles, stronger and more agile; the sense of touch, more meaningful. Early concepts are sensory concepts: *sights, sounds, feelings, manipulation.* The difference between senses used and senses ignored lies primarily in the meaning they will convey.[11] The more the senses are used and the more variety of stimulation they encounter, the more meaningful will be future sensory experiences with the environment. The urgency of this early training is exemplified in the fact that *during the first three years of life, the child develops fully 90 percent of his potential for visual perceptions.*[12] The future ability of the child to see *intelligently* will be largely determined by the experiences during the first three years of life. The amount of early stimulation the child receives prior to the age of three will, in large part, determine his visual success in subsequent years. The same basic principle holds true for the other senses.

These findings are very much in line with the research of Piaget. The more the child is placed in the position where he can accommodate his mental processes to the stimuli in the environment and the greater the variety and quantity of learnings assimilated, the more active and complete will be his environment. One thing seems to be apparent: *there can only be positive effects of early environmental stimulation, as long as there is a supportive parent around to provide the human element in this early learning.* That is not to say that a program of environmental enrichment is simple to develop; it is hard work, but if one considers the possible payoffs, this work is more than worthwhile.

Active Exploration Begins

As soon as the child is able to get around on his own, a different sort of environment has to be created for him. It is no longer necessary for the adult to take such an active role in bringing everything to the child. From this point on, the child must be provided with an environment which will permit him to explore for himself. The child nearing his first birthday is at a very crucial stage in his development. He is becoming able to locomote freely and explore his immediate environment. He is extremely curious and easily lured by objects of striking shape or color. However, he is not yet totally coordinated or aware of environmental dangers. Great care must be taken when encouraging free exploration, for leaving the one-year-old child alone makes him susceptible to possible injury or frustration. The adult must be a very skillful environmental designer, if the natural urges of the child are to be encouraged. The challenge is to construct an environment for the child which is at once stimulating and safe.[13] The child should always be made to feel that his creative explorations are being encouraged and certainly not made to feel guilty for what only comes naturally.

Many observers feel that the period between ten and eighteen months is the most significant single period in the child's total development.[14] Whether or not this is indeed the case is problematical, but the extreme importance of this period cannot be overestimated. It is during this period that the child is becoming more independent and developing a sense of self; he is rapidly becoming a person. The world is less of a nebulous void and is becoming more of a challenge than a mystery.

The newly achieved concept of object permanence has given the child a sense of reality.[15] He is recognizing the existence of a world apart from himself that will endure even when he is not present. This construction of an objective reality goes together with an increasing notion of self-importance. The more the child is encouraged to explore, the more comprehensive will be his world view and the better he will feel about himself. If exploration of his environment is unduly restricted, the child will feel less of a desire to follow his natural curiosity. This will not allow him to feel satisfied as an autonomous individual.

Early Speech Emerges

Another important development of this period is the emergence of early speech.[16] The young child is attracted to sound as well as to visual stimulation. As soon as he realizes that he too can make sounds, he tries to imitate the adult model. He begins to react to certain words spoken to him and is very sensitive to adult feelings in terms of vocal inflections. This is an ideal opportunity for the adult to use speech to reinforce the child's own investigations. Talking with children is an important aspect of intellectual development. For instance, if a child is exploring a box, it is helpful for the adult to vocalize *box*. Not only will the child probably be reinforced for his explorations by this form of attention, but he may also begin to associate the word with the object. A word of caution is in order here: using early language stimulation for purposes of reinforcement is good, but drilling the young child in language is not recommended. This type of drill will invariably confuse the child who is not yet ready to use language meaningfully.

The important thing in terms of experience at this age is that stimulation is increased as the child becomes ready for greater intensity of experience. In many underdeveloped nations, young children are given a tremendous amount of early stimulation.[17] As a result, the children are remarkable in terms of their intellectual development. However, due to the lack of educational opportunities, they tend to suffer intellectual deterioration in subsequent years. This is indeed one of the tragedies of world poverty. This lesson is an extremely important one: excessive stimulation is not advisable, because what is important is that the child receive a steadily increasing degree of independence and stimulation. This situation is similar to the one in which the serious athlete finds himself. The long-distance runner, for example, must pace himself in order to be able to cover the full distance as fast as possible. So it is with the young child who should be paced by the parent for optimal stimulation in order to maximize growth potential.

During the second year, the child becomes the master of the holophrase, the agrammatical one- or two-word utterance. *Allgone, upthere, mommy-byebye, wantthat,* and similar expressions become part of the fledgling vocabulary of the young child. Where in the past the child had to be brought stimulation he can now begin to ask for it. The child, at this age, also begins to ask, "What is that?" and is starting to recognize types and classes of things. This is extremely important to concept development, for it is through this embryonic language testing that the child becomes able to communicate and becomes a social being. The parent should take very great care to encourage the child and respond to his developing tendency to question and name things and to explore the usefulness of language.

The Child Experiments

The child is obtaining a tremendous amount of information, some of it erroneous. He is testing, adjusting his ideas and observations, and constantly associating sensory impressions with objects. He is forming basic, concrete concepts and is trying to fit all his new observations into these categories. The results are sometimes very humorous. Milton Young tells of the three year old who informed her family that her teacher was God.[18] Her mother had great difficulty accepting this and explained that it was not so. "Yes, she is God," the child exclaimed. "She brings us our juice, and we sit down and say, 'Thank you, God.' " The child is constantly trying to fit every piece of new information into some kind of associative and logical structure. The important thing to remember is *a single experience, no matter how rich, is not enough of a foundation upon which to build a concept.* The dissonance or puzzlement of the child, as in the above example, forces the child to recognize that there are multiple explanations for things, not just the most obvious one. Such situations, if handled delicately and maturely, teach the child to keep his concepts open and available for revision. Otherwise, concepts can become rigid and unchanging.

During the first four years of life, the child's creative imagination steadily increases up to a peak at around 4 or 4½ years, according to Paul Torrance, who has devoted much of his life to the study of creativity.[19] It is sometimes ignored that the very basis of perception is a creative activity:

the constructing of a unified impression of the world on the basis of isolated sensory stimuli. Perception is the raw material of all thinking: *sensations* create *percepts* which in time merge into *concepts.* Percepts of form merge into concepts of form; percepts of weight merge into concepts of *light* and *heavy;* percepts of taste merge into concepts of *sweet* and *sour;* and percepts of personal effectiveness merge into the fundamental concept of *self.*

From these early beginnings, tremendous achievements occur. The child becomes a person, an individual; he becomes free to explore, to roam, to create his own unique world and self-concept. The child is, to a large extent, an autonomous learner, but he must be presented with the material with which he forms associations and subsequent concepts. Exploration, if encouraged, will yield huge dividends in intellectual growth. The importance of this early experience is highlighted by Hunt's finding that, within certain, rough, predetermined limits, there are great differences due to environmental stimulation and Bloom's finding that about 50 percent of adult I.Q. is determined by the age of four and about 80 percent, by the age of eight.[20] The implications of these influential findings should be clear.

8

Early Learning Abilities

Perception

Our senses are the avenues of our experience. We can never remember not seeing, or not hearing, or not smelling, or not tasting, or not being able to touch and manipulate the world around us. It is only those who have experienced the diminution of some sensory capability who can really appreciate the importance of all of our senses to our well-being and efficient living. Our perceptual abilities are the greatest abilities that we have, and yet there are so many misconceptions about their development. Although we are normally born with eyes that work, with ears that can hear, with a mouth that can taste, with a nose that can smell, and with skin that has feeling for the textures and other sensations of the world around us, there is another element in human perception that is frequently ignored. This is the importance of experience. No matter how sensitive our sensory receptors are from our earliest days of life, we are unable to interpret the information which arrives at the brain, having been transmitted through the neural system from our sensory receptors. Without experience, the efficiency of our senses means almost nothing.[1]

Perhaps the most interesting evidence of this fact was provided by von Senden who studied the visual perception of a man who had been blind from birth and finally regained his sight in adulthood. The newly sighted man was found to have acute vision, but he had great difficulty "perceiving" the world. Certainly he could "see," but perception is much more than "sight" or "hearing" or "touch"; it is the interpretation of sense data on the basis of the rules derived through personal experience. The subject in von Senden's study could see, but he had not yet had the opportunity to learn the rules of visual perception.[2]

The infant, endowed with normal sensory apparatus, can see soon after birth, and see quite efficiently at that. However, the infant must learn how to interpret what she sees. She must learn to discriminate a foreground object from a background object; she must learn the nature of depth perception; and she must learn to interpret movement, along with other lessons. At birth, the difficult job of learning to perceive has just begun. It is not the kind of lesson that has to be specifically taught; it must be learned through personal experience with the physical world. There is much evidence to indicate that the more sensory experience the young child has, the better her perceptual abilities will develop, and the better able she will be to perceive and deal with the world.[3]

The development of visual ability (usually called *visual acuity,* or sharpness of vision) occurs rather rapidly after birth.[4] At first the infant may only use one eye, but vision with two eyes follows after a week or two of life. Within two months, the infant is able to direct her eyes toward objects directly in front of her or those dangling directly above her. As an object is moved, the newborn has difficulty following it, but this ability soon becomes part of her visual repertoire. It is interesting to watch the development of the infant's reactions to movement, at first rather uncoordinated and then becoming increasingly controlled. After a while, the infant will become able to fix her gaze on moving objects most anywhere within her limited visual field. These first few months are important ones for the infant as she becomes increasingly able to control her perceptual abilities.[5]

During these first few months, the infant does not see the world very clearly. She is still learning to interpret the visual sensations that bombard her constantly. Objects and people remain relatively undifferentiated patterns of light. The mother has not yet been perceived as a person or a unified entity; she is still just a combination of sensations: visual sensations, auditory sensations, tactile sensations, and olfactory sensations. These first sensations and perceptions are very pleasurable, and the young infant thrives on perceptual experience and sensory stimulation.[6]

Soon the infant begins to recognize recurring perceptual patterns. She needs the security or repetition, but, interestingly enough, it has been found that infants also thrive on novelty. Most often attributed to the experimental work of Hebb[7] and Berlyne,[8] the discovery of the early desire and preference for novelty and complexity has profoundly affected our views of early childhood. In essence, psychologists have found, and continue to find, that young children, almost from birth, tend to seek novelty and complexity and react very favorably to them. Research has indicated that this could account for the infant's fascination with the human face, a relatively complex visual form.[9] In addition, experiments have shown that the young infant prefers patterned forms to simple forms, and her early concentration on these forms has been shown to be truly remarkable.[10] Much of the research into the preference for complexity in infants has been carried out by Fantz.[11] This research has contributed to the popular view that the newborn is an active perceiver and a highly motivated learner. All this young learner seems to require is the opportunity to exercise her perceptual skills.

Sensory stimulation and opportunities for early perceptual experience, furthermore, allow the infant to integrate her perceptual images. The child who gets little attention and does not have the opportunity to integrate this sensory data has been shown to be at a great disadvantage. Indeed, there is some evidence that this lack of early perceptual experience may be difficult to overcome. The reason for this belief is that perceptual learning, like most other learning, is hierarchical (each succeeding bit depends upon previous bits). When an uneven foundation has been laid, there is some doubt about the stability of the subsequent structure.[12]

Developmental Trends in Human Perception

The perceptual field of the child becomes wider and wider.[13] Through maturity and experience, the young child develops an increasingly large world. No matter how large an infant's environment might be, it is tiny until the child can attend to it and interpret it. At first, she can see very little except what is directly in front of her; gradually, the field of perception increases. Although this will happen naturally to some extent, perceptual experience will speed the process and bring it to a higher level of ultimate development. Assistance can come through the provision of an array of moving objects and other stimuli. Even moving in and out of the infant's visual field can help the child exercise her broadening and maturing ability to perceive a wider and wider portion of her environment.

The child develops a greater span of attention.[14] At first, the infant's attention is quite diffuse. The world is so new and rich that it takes some time for the child to begin fixating her attention on specific aspects of the environment. In addition, the infant is quite easily distracted. This is not bad; it is quite natural. Distraction should not be avoided. Through experience with a variety of objects and other stimuli, the child will develop a greater ability to fix her attention on specific sights and sounds. In essence, the infant gradually develops greater "selectivity" of attention. A variety of environmental stimulation will help the child along the way to greater attention and concentration.

The child becomes less bound to specific stimuli in her perceptual activities.[15] She begins to search more actively for stimulation and explore her visual field. At first, her perceptual world is virtually limited to items placed directly within her sight. Eventually, the infant develops the ability to look and listen on her own and decide what to look at and what to ignore. The addition of stimulation above and beyond the immediate perceptual field can aid the child in overcoming initial dependency on stimuli directly in front of her.

The child gradually develops greater perceptual flexibility.[16] She learns how to explore with her senses and is able to perceive numerous different characteristics of people and objects. The child develops less desire to concentrate on one aspect of a stimulus and begins to explore things more comprehensively. Soon she becomes a "perceptual detective," and this independent perceptual investigation is wonderful to watch. It is through this more advanced exploration that the child begins to piece together the diverse characteristics of her perceived world. Perceptual flexibility, gained largely through experience, is a key development in the child's perceptual and intellectual growth processes.

The child's perception becomes increasingly differentiated.[17] It is a major step from seeing clearly to being able to perceive discrete aspects of the sensory world. At first, the young infant perceives a mass of color, shape, lines, sounds, tastes, touch, and other undifferentiated sensory impressions. Although "in focus" soon after birth, these sensory impressions do not yet mean anything to the child. At first the sensory world is a mass of confusion, although a very exciting mass of confusion! Soon the child begins the arduous task of bringing together the diverse impressions of the world into coherent images. Shapes begin to have meaning; from lines, the child begins to infer depth; the world is soon viewed as being composed of separate regions; colors are differentiated, as are brightness and hue.

Objects in the visual field develop characteristics of permanency and constancy.[18] At first, the child does not realize that perception is more than that which is immediately perceived. Even though the child is not looking at something, it is still "there."[19] With maturation and familiarization with the immediate physical environment, the young child is soon able to begin the difficult job of constructing a coherent and unified reality. This development has a great deal to do with the child's developing objectivity, and the beginning realization that the world is not just an appendage of her being. Although this development usually is firmly established near the end of the first year of life, it can begin much sooner. In addition, the child learns of perceptual constancies. Color, for instance, remains the same under different light conditions; shape does not change even though one might be viewing something from a different angle (and it might appear to change); size of objects does not change when you get closer or farther away. However, the newborn does not know these things. Because the infant is dependent upon "appearance," she needs time and a great deal of experience to learn these perceptual constancies.

Organization of Perceptual Experience

Why do some people process information and learn more efficiently than others? Certainly part of the answer to this important question is attributable to differentials in early perceptual experiences. We know that some people have certain perceptual strengths. We all acknowledge that the painter is particularly adept at "seeing" his visual world; the musician, at hearing; the blind man, at touching; the gourmet chef, at tasting and smelling. It is highly unlikely that these people are born with these sensory gifts; a more likely explanation is that they are developed through hard work and extensive experience.

In essence, the process of perception is very much a type of "concept formation."[20] Through experience with different sensations, we build perceptual categories under which we group different aspects of our experience. The efficiency with which we interpret the data from our sense organs depends, in large part, upon the richness of our prior experience. The young child has little experience, and her primary developmental task is exploration. If we have had a rich and varied experience with the color green, subsequent experiences with this color will be very meaningful to us. Obviously the painter has tended to focus his attention upon the basic characteristics of the visual world: colors, lines, and shapes. The gourmet chef has concentrated his attention upon the characteristics of the food he prepares; thus, certain tastes and smells have deep meaning for him. The same holds true for other examples of perceptual development. Although certain perceptual facility comes naturally, some people are not willing to accept abilities that are "just adequate."

Perhaps the most intriguing characteristic of human perception is its *selectivity*.[21] From the huge smorgasbord of perceptual sensations, we can choose those to which we want to attend and tune out those we don't.

It is just not possible to attend to every sensation. It is by necessity that we must exercise this "selective perception" ability. At first, the child has little choice; she will attend to the stimulus that attracts her attention. This type of early perceptual selectivity is essentially passive. Later, as the child develops more of a sense of personal determinism and objectivity, she will begin to consciously select the objects of her perception. Just as we try to repeat experiences that we have found interesting and pleasurable (games, foods, artistic pleasures, etc.), so do we tend to perceive those things that have given us happiness in the past.

It is truly remarkable the way humans learn to organize their experiences. Experience breeds experience, and, in perception, similar experiences tend to attract and organize each other. The organization of our experiences into conceptual and perceptual categories is a result of the combined efforts of all our intellectual abilities, a coordinated effort of all we have learned thus far. If category formation is to be satisfactory, children need practice in using their senses. Since our senses are the "doors to our mind," sensory experience is crucial to all learning.

Obviously, the average person is not going to be as observant as the painter, as sharp at hearing as the musician, as adept at touch as the sculptor, or as sensitive to smell and taste as the gourmet chef. However, the average person can be *perceptually well rounded* as compared with any of these people who specialize in limited sensory abilities. Rarely do we hear of the exceptional talent who is well rounded in all areas of human endeavor. In order to develop exceptional skills, it is sometimes necessary to trade ability and experience in some areas for others. In the long run, this balanced, sensory development will produce an individual who is able to process a wide variety of information efficiently.

One of the chief reasons for developing all the senses is the fact that our senses are all closely interrelated and interdependent, and together they form our complete human perceptual system. As we experience our world, we are forming combined sensory impressions based on present and past experience with the object under consideration and including data from all our senses. If sensory information is lacking, our sensory impressions will be less complete, and our experience with that object will consequently be less meaningful.

In a very real sense, perception "compresses" information about the outside world.[22] What we see, hear, feel, smell, and taste is but a sample of all sensations that are available to us. Through perception we extract or abstract distinctive features from our environment, features which we have come to consider to be important in dealing with specific situations. The human perceptual system is a "limited-capacity system" and cannot cope with every sensation that is available for us to perceive. We must compress the information of the real world in order to cope with it effectively. The process that we use to compress the information that bombards our senses is similar to that used in concept formation: we select features of the environment to which we choose to attend and ignore those which are irrelevant. In concept formation, we form categories by abstracting *distinctive features* in order to organize our experiences. This is also what our senses do through experience and practice. It should be recognized that, just as in concept formation, the more experience we have, the more efficient will be our perceptual functioning, and the more effectively we will be able to deal with the complexity of our environment.

Research indicates that the early years of life are the most advantageous for perceptual learning. This is because the young child can learn most productively in this way.[23] Up until the age of 1½ or 2 years, the very young child is at a stage of development which Piaget calls the sensorimotor stage. She is learning about objects and exploring them with her senses. Later in life, learning becomes primarily a mental activity, involving language more than actual concrete experience. If sensory and perceptual learning is not forthcoming at an early age, it may never come. *Sensory and perceptual learning is childhood learning.* It is vitally important that we train the "doors of the mind," for it is through them that all subsequent experiences must pass. And, because this learning is so basic and fundamental, we often tend to take it for granted. As a result, very few children or adults ever even approach the optimal level of sensory functioning.

Motor Abilities

Motor ability or movement is a much more fundamental aspect of human learning than most people realize. When most of us think about intellect or knowledge, we do not think about physical ability or motor coordination. However, human mental and physical abilities are closely related, and one is difficult to develop without the other.[24] Perception is the process of acquiring information from the environment; motor ability is involved in exploration of the environment and acting upon this information. Perceptual and motor abilities are almost completely interdependent, particularly in terms of early childhood learning. Actually when we think of sensory exploration, we must always consider motor skills. When we look at an object, we must move our bodies to explore it or manipulate it in some way. When we touch something, obviously movement is a very important part of the activity. Perhaps movement is less important as a prerequisite ability for hearing, smell, and taste than for sight and touch, but certainly it is important for every type of exploratory activity.

Motor ability is absolutely crucial. It is the close link between perceptual and motor learning that has caused many observers to refer to human perceptual learning as *perceptual-motor learning.* An understanding of the important link between perception and manipulation will come from just observing an infant for a few moments as she explores an object. The movement of the head, the shoulders, the mouth, the arms, the fingers in relation to visual exploration all attest to the importance of physical coordination in perception.[25] For, without this coordination, the information which is available to the senses will be extremely limited. In addition, the success that a young child has in these early active explorations of the environment will, to a great extent, determine her psychological well-being and self-concept, as well as the meaningfulness of the information that she will derive from these explorations.

Through continual experience, the child develops movement patterns. Initially, movement is reflective and relatively uncontrolled, but, through practice and physical maturation, the child learns to coordinate movements into patterns. She learns through trial-and-error exploration, practice, and, sometimes, specific training to associate certain movements with each other and to coordinate these movements with vision in order to accomplish a manipulative task. Motor learning progresses from grosser to finer abilities. It takes time and practice before fine manipulative abilities are learned. As the child learns manipulative skills, she will also learn to coordinate perceptual and motor abilities.

Physical maturation occurs in two directions: from shoulder to finger and from head to toe. This means that the young child is able to move her head and shoulders before she is able to coordinate her hands or walk. As a result of this direction of physical and motor development, activities aimed at enriching perceptual-motor experience should be restricted to activities for which the child is physically ready. This is a point that the adult intuitively knows, since physical readiness is more obvious than mental readiness. However, due to the importance of motor activity for development and, in early childhood, for competence and self-concept, this point cannot be overemphasized.

The child should have an opportunity to manipulate a wide variety of different materials. In motor ability, as well as in other areas of human endeavor, most learning derives from direct experience. The broader this experience, the firmer will be the foundation for future experience. The more varied the motor patterns that are developed, the more competent the child will become in the crucial area of perceptual-motor exploration. However, great care should be taken to ensure that activities are appropriate to the child's level of development. No matter how much practice or experience the young child has with a heavy weight, she will not be able to lift it. The point is very simply to give the child materials to manipulate that are not too big, too small, too heavy, or inappropriate in other ways for her level of functioning. Just as for all skills, motor skills are most efficient when they are hierarchical and are learned in a gradual progression from basic to complex skills. Furthermore, in order to encourage the child to develop her motor skills, material presented should be as interesting, colorful, and varied as possible. *Novelty appears to be the great motivator in all areas of early childhood learning.*

Memory

Memory is really the integration of all the elements discussed above. It is the cumulative effect of past experience.[26] However, this does not mean that we remember things "intact"; in fact, almost every experience changes previous experience by building upon it. Time and experience change and consolidate the information that we store in our memories. Perhaps the most important single determinant of what we remember is the *meaningfulness* of the information. We will remember best that which is meaningful to us on the basis of past experience and present cognitive organization. In essence, memory is a function of past experience, interpreted by cognitive structures, perceptual ability, sensory and motor integration, and the organization of specific concepts. Together those factors determine our ability to retain, organize, and use the information that is available to us.

The most basic learnings are perceptual learnings, such as form, color, texture, taste, and relationship to other things. These basic learnings are fundamental to subsequent experiences and, to a large extent, determine the meaningfulness of future experiences. Eventually, most learning is shifted from an emphasis on perception to an emphasis on language. From that point on, most learning becomes based on words and the meaningfulness of the words is largely assumed. Memory too becomes largely a verbal mechanism, and experiences become coded in the memory in the form of words. If our early perceptual experiences have been rich enough, then our language and verbal memory will be rich. When we hear a word used, we will have rich mental images or remembrances as a result. It is the fact that most memory becomes dependent upon language that makes early perceptual enrichment and sensory learning so important. As Woodruff has so cogently said, "verbal input can lead to concept maturation (growth) only when the essential bits of perceptual meaning are present."[27]

Memory Processes

Recognition is the most basic process in memory.[28] The very young child eventually develops this ability through continual experience and through the learning process of association. Recognition is an extremely important process because it provides the young child with the stability of perception necessary for building for herself an enduring world view. Recognition develops as experience progresses with the parents, common objects in the immediate environment, familiar surroundings, and familiar sounds. The more experience the young child has with her environment, the more that will become familiar to her and the more she will recognize. Recognition represents the primary mechanism for remembering until about the age of two, when the child becomes ready for higher forms of remembering.

Recall is the next advance in memory.[29] Recall is the ability not only to recognize but also to specifically retrieve pieces (bits) of information for use. Until the development of recall, the child is still very much dependent upon the present. With the development of recall, the child can begin to piece together the past and use it to anticipate the future. In addition, recall is absolutely essential for the beginnings of language development. It is at this stage that the child begins to imitate words and associate meaning with them. Specific language training has been started at this stage of development by a number of experimenters, but, although the child of two can learn language with extensive practice, there is no proven advantage for doing so. It has, in fact, been shown to inhibit the development of more appropriate learning, since early memory is very limited.

Recollection is an even more advanced level of memory.[30] It not only includes recall but is also predicated on the ability to group information meaningfully. Recollection is very similar in nature to the ability assumed in concept formation. It also means the ability to locate events and objects in space and time, and it marks the beginning of mature memory processes and of what can truly be considered to be "knowledge."

In summary, it is the efficiency of our perceptions and the organization of knowledge into concepts that determine the effectiveness and productivity of future experience. The entire process of storing information for future use is termed *memory,* and is determined by all the factors previously mentioned. In terms of memory ability, there is a long way to go from infancy to efficient storage of knowledge. However, that does not mean that certain prior achievements cannot be made. Perceptual-motor abilities and experience with a wide variety of environmental stimuli can precede mature mental processes and produce more optimal conditions for the higher-level functioning.

9

Visual Concepts

The human perceptual system is the greatest concept-forming agent there is, and the human eye is unrivaled as the foremost perceptual concept former. Our visual images have been synthesized from scattered sensory impressions on the basis of the stimulation of more than 100 million light-sensitive cells in the retina of the eye.[1] Stimulation of the retina is only indirectly related to what we actually "see." There is a long, intermediate process in which the sensory impressions are interpreted on the basis of experience and what we have learned. Indeed, seeing is not as automatic as one is led to believe through the apparent effortlessness of vision. What we actually see is in no way simply a mirror image of what exists in our visual world. Few of us realize the incredible complexity of the mental mechanisms that go into "piecing together" the visual image which we take for granted. The nature of the visual perception process can be understood better if we consider it in ten steps:

1. Motivation (need)	6. Sensation
2. Visual search or scanning	7. Consolidation of sensations
3. Attention	8. Interpretation
4. Visual exploration	9. Organization
5. Fixation	10. Conceptualization (completed image)

First, there must be a motivation or need for the individual to explore his visual world. He then searches his visual field employing scanning techniques, moving his eyes, his head, and, if necessary, his body. Third, he directs his attention to a specific area within his visual field and subsequently explores this area with his eyes, which are constantly in motion. The individual fixes his attention on a specific object or group of objects, and light reflected off these objects enters the eye where it is focused by the lens, directed toward light-sensitive cells of the retina, and causes a series of sensations. Seventh, these millions of sensations are consolidated as they are carried by nerve fibers to the brain, so that the sensory information will be manageable. The brain then interprets the information transported to it, attempting to construct a coherent image from all of this diverse information. Using perceptual principles, and past experience, the brain organizes the information. And, finally, a coherent visual image is constructed, a true concept in that it represents *a functional grouping experience.* Believe it or not, this is a highly simplified version of the process of visual perception.[2]

Certainly the ability of human beings to accomplish this extraordinary procedure so efficiently is magnificent, especially considering that the process occurs in thousandths of a second, thousands of times a day. It is through this unconscious process of conceptualization that we are able to exist in our visual world. However, some people live and operate more effectively than others, probably resulting from the learned ability of some people to synthesize perceptual information better than others. We can do little about improving the efficiency of our eyes, except perhaps to have regular eye examinations and purchase proper corrective lenses. However, there is plenty we can do to improve the efficiency of the brain in interpreting the information transported to it from our eyes, especially if this is done at an early age. Experience, both quantitative and qualitative, is the answer.[3]

Much of the content of this discussion has been inspired by Rudolf Arnheim, who has devoted much of his life to the study of the visual powers of man.[4] Arnheim's concerns have never been with mere eyesight; his concerns are with "visual thinking," the higher-level interpretation of visual information. Arnheim believes that the process of visual perception "anticipates in a modest way the admired capacity of the artist to produce patterns that validly interpret experience by means of organized form."[5]

According to Arnheim, form is the perceptual carrier of meaning and the beginning of man's visual concepts.[6] The importance of form as a visual concept can be understood if you consider why a child does not draw a circle to represent a human head and an adult usually does. The child is drawing what he sees, an irregular oval shape. The adult is drawing a visual category which has come to represent a human head *by convention.*[7] Look at another example. If one drew a picture that looked like a human heart, it would be very difficult for the observer to comprehend what it was out of context. Yet, when one draws a symbolic heart shape like this ♡ , everybody knows that he is trying to represent a heart in visual form. The mind works very much like this in interpreting visual information. It interprets sensations on the basis of past experience and learned conventions. If we have had a great deal of anatomical experience with investigating the human head, we might view it, in our mental imagination, as being irregular, unique to the individual, and specific in shape. If we had learned a great deal of biology, we may be more realistic in our rendering of the human heart. However, most of us *simplify* visual images into a form which we can readily use, communicate, and efficiently deal with. Much like the word concepts we explored earlier, our visual impressions and sensations are usually formed into visual concepts, represented by a mental symbol or stereotyped image.

Visual Processes

In addition to this *simplification* on the basis of generalized form, the human perceptual system transforms raw sensations in other ways such as *selection, completion, comparison,* and *interpreting in relation to context.* [8] These important processes involved in visual concept formation will be briefly discussed in turn.

Simplification

Simplification refers to the human perceptual tendency to see things in their simplest form. It is much like the process of the abstraction of concept attributes discussed earlier, whereby distinctive features of classes of objects are isolated, and all such objects become members of equivalent classes. Normally, when we see our world, we do not see all the unique aspects of the things around us for reasons of perceptual economy. If we were to view each distinctive feature of every part of our field of vision, we would be lost in a needless proliferation of irrelevant detail. In almost every way, our perceptual system acts as a very effective agent of conceptualization. However, just as there is the possibility of overgeneralization and overconceptualization, there is also the possibility of oversimplifying our visual world. This is precisely what occurs in very many cases. By oversimplifying things, we fail to see, understand, and appreciate the uniqueness and beauty around us. The child who has been taught and allowed to explore everything in his environment, not only with his eyes, but with all his senses, will probably be able to develop more of an appreciation for his visual world later in life. This is the development of meaningful concepts, visual or otherwise. Everybody, by necessity, develops categories of experience, but some people are able to develop more meaningful categories than others *on the basis of more extensive experience* as well as *multisensory exploration and inquiry.*[9] Simplification of our world into visual categories need not preclude the richness of these categories.

Selection

Selection is the tendency of humans to choose the aspects of their environment to which they wish to attend. Actually, selection and simplification usually operate together, as people selectively choose the attributes of objects upon which they base their simplification. It is perhaps the most fundamental aspect of human perception that people tend to view or listen to what they want to see or hear. When we see something we do not like, we have the ability, called selective perception, to look away or look at something else. When we hear something we do not like, we can concentrate on something else or "tune it out." The human perceptual ability to select stimuli from the environment is one of the most interesting characteristics of human beings. It is also potentially one of the most creative, for it allows us greater freedom of exploration and investigation. The selectivity of our vision is *perceptual freedom,* if we use it as such.

Completion

Completion is the tendency of human perception to complete an unfinished view of something. We cannot see everything every time we glance at an area in our field of vision, and yet our mental image of a scene is always complete. It is a fact that we rarely see every part of most objects, but we see them as they are because we complete them from memory. Humans cannot tolerate incomplete perceptions. This may relate to our misinterpretation of sensory data in that we may complete a world view with something which was not really there but has been associated with it in our memory.

Comparison

Comparison refers to the important human perceptual trait of viewing the world relatively, not absolutely. Most people see shape relative to other shapes and color relative to other colors and evaluate them as such. One figure is rounder than another, or squarer. One object is brighter than another, or heavier. Through experience we have learned to compare objects very efficiently. Distance is another perceptual attribute that is almost always measured relatively. When we say that something is brown or large or far, we are saying this relative to other similar instances we have experienced. Some of the most important concept adjectives we learn are *relational,* or comparative. It is extremely important that we learn to make comparisons objectively, intelligently, and on the basis of sound evidence. For it is these comparative judgments that help us orient ourselves to other things within our visual world. We should place more emphasis than we do on teaching children to effectively deal with these important relational concepts.[10]

Context Interpretation

Finally, there is the fact that we interpret every piece of perceptual data according to the context in which it occurs. A table in a home will be viewed differently than a table in an antique gallery. The former will probably be viewed more for its functional value, and the latter, more for its aesthetic value. The color green may be viewed differently when surrounded by red than when surrounded by yellow. A light color will look lighter on a black background than it will on a white background. You might want to try out these situations, and variations of them, to help you understand this important perceptual principle. This principle and the principle of comparison are closely related and aid us in understanding the importance of teaching children that everything is relative, a subjective judgment of placing things on a scale between zero and infinity. The more successful we are in these judgments, the better our visual orientation to our world will be.

Summary

So it is with all our senses. We simplify, select, complete, compare, and consider the context in interpreting perceptual stimuli. Rarely do we do any of these things consciously, but we always do them. It is the unconscious nature of these operations that makes it so imperative that we help our children to do these things effectively. Perceptual education must come early in the child's life. The very young child, during the period of natural curiosity and active sensory exploration, can learn these things very easily. In fact, he can learn them without any instruction at all, simply through repeated and rich experience with the raw material of perceptual concepts: shape, color, texture, weight, smell, and other sensations. It is important to realize that everything the child sees and does is based on the ability to interpret perceptual data effectively.

This chapter has dealt with what Rudolf Arnheim calls "intelligent perception"; it is the recognition of the reality of our perceptual processes and our mastery of them.[11] Vision can be free and active, or it can become accustomed to go only where it is led. Advertisers spend millions of dollars to discover new ways to enslave our perceptions and the perceptions of our children, to direct our attention for us, and to cater to unintelligent perception. This need not be the case. We must be aware of the necessity of experience in perception for, without meaning brought by experience, our perceptions can be as empty as memorized words. This being so, our perceptions can be easily manipulated by others.

It should be understood that visual information is the predominant type. We may hear, touch, smell, and taste, but we always see as well. Fully 85 percent of our perceptual information intake is visual, and efficiency of processing such information is imperative.[12]

10

Learning
and Play

Although not commonly thought of as such, play can be the most useful context for early childhood education.[1] Play is active, fun, manipulative, dynamic; it can provide the child with the opportunity to experiment, to test new ideas, and to attain mastery without having to also cope with the complexity of reality. Play can provide the proper mix between serious learning and enjoyment. The parent or teacher who drills the child in skills, without injecting an element of fun into the situation, will probably turn the child off to future learning. Whenever possible, early learning and play should be one and the same. There is no more valuable early childhood development than the discovery that play can be creative and that learning can be fun. This development can lead the child to greater and greater intellectual achievements. The parent who treats play as being predominantly a mindless activity and frequently a waste of time will probably instill those beliefs in the child, while the adult who understands the importance of *meaningful* play will encourage the child to learn while having fun. The importance of this fact should become clear when viewing a creative person at work. Such a person is usually able to merge the world of play with the world of work.[2] This marriage of work and play usually must begin in early childhood, when, under the proper conditions and support, hard work in learning can become a joyous activity. *Most of the activities suggested in this book are designed to foster this connection between learning and play.* However, ultimately, the most significant influence in the child's linking of learning and play will be the parents' and teachers' supportive role in the process. The adult who is able to enjoy the learning process *with* the child and the adult who also himself knows the joy of learning will be the ultimate determinant of whether learning and play become equated in the child's mind.

Understanding Childhood Play

Novelty and Curiosity

Essential to the understanding of childhood play is the notion of *curiosity*. Researchers have found curiosity to be an extremely important psychological factor in all higher animals, including man.[3] There is something about novelty that seems to create interest, motivation, and exploratory behavior. The lure of the new is not restricted to the inventor or the explorer; everyone possesses some of the venturesome characteristics of these people.[4] Interest is provoked by the new and different, while our attention and perceptions are dulled by the routine and commonplace. Newness should be presented in appropriate quantities, without overwhelming the organism. *If too much is routine, we are bored; but if too much is new, then we can become lost.*[5] It is a tremendous challenge indeed for the parent or teacher to provide an adequate degree of novelty in order to inspire curiosity, without providing so much that meaning cannot be made of it.

One of the most potent characteristics of play activities is the amount of novelty which can be generated. If play activities are properly developed, the child cannot only be exposed to a wide variety of stimuli, but she can also generate a tremendous variety of combinations, problems, solutions, or perspectives herself. The child can be creative; she can do things which are not permitted in real life, with its reality-based constraints. The child can satisfy her wishes, longings, requirement for novelty, creative impulses, and other natural psychological needs of early childhood. Play can provide an opportunity for the child to experiment, to learn the importance of her own ideas, to have fun, to be curious, and to explore. Play provides opportunities for the child which no other aspect of life can equal. But play is serious business and should be understood by those who use it; it should be a source of great pleasure for both adult and child. It should be a time for creativity, exploration, and joy, *without* the need for evaluation, judgment, or criticism.

Fantasy

Fantasy is one of the most significant aspects of childhood.[6] Fantasy is the opportunity for the child to release herself of the pressures of reality and to imagine, to create, and to consider things which are not obtainable to her in reality. Fantasy is an attribute of the psychologically healthy child.[7] The parent who encourages fantasy and imagination will provide the child with the motivation to extend her imaginative thinking to aspects of the real world. The parent who discourages this creative thinking will cause the child to feel guilty for doing what only comes naturally and will inhibit her natural impulses. Adults sometimes fail to realize that children actually have few opportunities to express themselves creatively. While adults can undertake creative activities whenever they wish because they have the power to control their own lives, children are dependent, and their creative behavior must usually take the form of fantasy or play. Although there is no scientific evidence, many observers have hypothesized that one of the primary differences between creative and noncreative adults is the degree of early encouragement of fantasy and play.[8] Modes of thinking are usually established quite early in life, and the encouragement of imagination, as well as the lack of evaluative criticism of the young child's ideas, can provide a model of behavior which will endure throughout an entire lifetime.

Although fantasy is usually an individual activity, the same type of freewheeling thought that is present in fantasy can carry over to play activities between parent and child, as well as affect other aspects of life. Imagination, creativity, curiosity, deferred evaluation, understanding, and encouragement should always be part of the play situation. Moreover, there is no reason why play activities cannot be *structured* in some specific way to encourage these qualities. Most of the "games" suggested in this book have a specific purpose, a specified lesson or stimulation which is intended to result. However, most of these activities are designed in such a way that the child can respond "correctly" *in any number of different ways,* particularly in the beginning stages of each activity. There is no need for evaluation for there is no specific response that is required, and the child is free to respond individualistically and creatively. This should be the key notion of learning through play for the very young child: *play activities should not often require a specified response.* If the play activity does encourage a specific response, it may not provide the child with an opportunity for creativity and self-expression, may cause the child to think in a single way, and will, by its very nature, encourage the adult to evaluate the child's response in adult terms.

Characteristics of Play

Play provides the child with an opportunity to solve problems. One of the most invigorating feelings for any human being, adult or child, is to have solved a problem, invented something, or experienced insight. Jerome Bruner, the influential psychologist, has said that education should be the process of constantly reinventing ideas and information.[9] Certainly, we cannot all be great geniuses and inventors, but we can be provided with a context in which we can rediscover the great ideas of the past and gain great satisfaction in the process. A child can rediscover the ideas of Gallileo, Copernicus, and Einstein given an appropriate situation, proper clues, and motivation. *Education should be a process of rediscovery.*[10] We fail sometimes to realize that, although an idea may not be new to the world, it is new to the child. When the child has discovered it, the feeling of accomplishment and ecstasy is equalled by no other learning experience. If the play situation is properly designed so that the child is carefully led toward a solution, or one of the many solutions, the learning that can result is incredible. This is one of the objectives of the exercises in this book: promoting insight and creative problem solving. If the child is gradually led toward the discovery and rediscovery of information, she will experience the ultimate joy of learning.

Play also provides an opportunity for the child to achieve competence. Robert White has formulated a theory of "competence motivation," the extremely important notion that children need to achieve a feeling of competence, or mastery, in order to feel adequate, successful, and complete as human beings.[11] Competence is closely linked to the notion of esteem. The more competent the child feels and the more others reinforce her competence, the more complete will be her sense of self-concept. Since the child is so dependent, she has few opportunities to demonstrate her competence. Montessori has stressed the important idea of giving the child opportunities to learn practical skills as soon as possible: dressing, cleanliness, chores, etc.[12] But play is the most important early opportunity for achieving childhood competence. Competence is a total feeling of self-effectiveness, and play is an important step toward this feeling.

Play provides the child with a chance, perhaps her only chance, to formulate, discover, and design her own rules. Interestingly enough, Vygotsky has described play as an activity in which there are definite rules, a point that is often neglected by those who feel that play is totally free and undisciplined.[13] In fact, play is the first opportunity of the child to place restrictions on herself, without having to depend solely upon the external discipline of adults. When the child is able to understand the goal of the "game," she will devise strategies, rules, and principles for achieving it, especially if the activity is important to her in some way. Self-discipline is an important lesson, and purposeful play can greatly contribute toward its learning.

Play can increase the attention span of the child. One of the key deficiencies of the young child is her lack of attention. This does not necessarily mean that there is a behavior problem, for the young child constantly has new things competing for her attention, and she is easily distracted.[14] The play situation, with just the right amount of repetition and variety, can train the child to concentrate longer and longer on activities. Some children never learn the important lesson of concentration, even on entering formal schooling, and this indeed is sad. No matter how intelligent a child is, if she is unable to concentrate on things and give her attention, she will not be a successful learner or person. Sometimes there is a perceptual problem (and the exercises in this book will deal with the training of perceptual ability), but usually problems of attention are due merely to lack of practice. Like most learning, attention and concentration must be practiced, yet that does not mean forcing the child to pay attention. The child's attention should be seduced by the situation.

Play is interesting and dynamic. One of the often overlooked aspects of play is its dynamic quality.[15] It is always changing. If a game is worth playing, it permits the player to react differently most every time it is played. The popularity of games such as chess and bridge is probably due, in large part, to the fact that there are so many possible situations which can occur and moves that can be made. Certainly childhood games cannot be as sophisticated or complex as these, but that does not mean that we cannot learn from adult games. It has been conclusively proven by researchers that the more complex a stimulus, the more interested the child will be in it; the more a situation changes, the more compelling it will be.[16] It is important not to present the child with play situations which are static, which do not permit the child to react differently from time to time. If play is static, it will become tedious. Novelty is a key element of all aspects of life and the more novelty we create, the better prepared children will be for a complex world, and the more excited and interested they will be in learning and discovering new things.

Summary

Play is not easy, if it is to be a worthwhile experience. The great play situation is a work of art. It should be designed for those who will be playing it, and be geared to their specific characteristics. It should provide the opportunity for the solving of relevant and appropriate problems. Play should be a process of discovery and rediscovery. It should stress the notion of competence, physical and intellectual. It should encourage the player to devise her own rules and strategies as much as possible. It should encourage attention through its dynamic quality of change. And, perhaps most important, play should be interesting and fun. Children should never be forced to play, and they should never be required to participate longer at an activity than they wish. When the child becomes restless, let her do something else. Play should be joyous, and learning through play should be a constant revelation.

11

The Role of
the Adult

The role of the parent and teacher in facilitating the development of the young child is basically threefold: *motivator, organizer,* and *evaluator.* However, it is the child who must be the "doer." The adult should prepare the child for experiences, organize these experiences in such a way that they will be most beneficial, help the child evaluate his success, and help him discover new ways to experience reality.

The Need for Esteem

The need for esteem, self-esteem and the esteem of others, is perhaps the most important human motive. Esteem is not love, but respect; respect for competence, mastery, and ability. Satisfying these needs is the very basis of the child's self-concept. The young child desperately strives for esteem, and the surest way to it is through competence, as demonstrated by success in developmental tasks.[1] The child who performs well in his exploration of the environment will achieve this esteem and be reinforced in his future explorations. During these important early stages of development, adults should manage the natural inquiry of the child so as to assure his successful attainment of esteem, especially self-esteem.

Motivation is basic to the individual, but it must be directed and satisfied.[2] The normal child strives most often to satisfy the basic need for esteem. The first method for assuring that the child will satisfy this need is by making the child think that his ideas are important and that the problems he faces are of significant proportions. The surest way of deflating the child's ego is failure at an easy task. The adult should help the child recognize the significance of his little tasks, for these tasks are not so little to him. The first rule of motivational management is *Little problems seem big to little people.* As long as the child is helped by the parent to realize that the problems he faces are substantial and important, he will not be easily frustrated, even in temporary failure.

The young child is constantly questioning, reaching out for answers, and exploring the newness of the world. *The parent or teacher should never make the child feel that his questions are unimportant, unintelligent, or a nuisance.*[3] Questions are the child's way of making sense of his world. His question may be agrammatical, simplistic, ill defined, and immature; but it must always be considered valid and important. Children's questions that go unanswered or are berated will probably be translated into a feeling of failure and lack of worth.

Active Learning

The next important consideration for the adult is that *knowledge which is left unused is frustrating.* There must be adequate opportunities for the child to act upon what he has learned. In earlier chapters, great emphasis was placed on the constant learning that takes place during early childhood. Such learning can overwhelm the child with information, unless there are outlets for practical use. It is undeniable that children today are information rich and action poor; they have so much learning thrust at them, but rarely get the opportunity to use their new knowledge. The active learning that will be described in later chapters is a response to this problem. Parents and teachers should recognize the need of children to actively manipulate and work with information, not just assimilate it. Learning activities that allow active participation on the child's part will help him gain a sense of self-esteem, pleasure, and satisfaction of having done something creative and tangible. There is no more satisfying human accomplishment than creativity, and there is no reason why the child cannot be made to feel its rewards through the facilitation of such accomplishment.

Tasks must be brought down to the size of the child in order to assure success. Montessori felt that the best way to assure success for the child was to create a child-sized environment with chairs, tables, and other objects appropriate to the size of the child.[4] Perhaps all this is unnecessary, but it is necessary for the parent to provide the child with tasks that will not frustrate or overwhelm him. *Teaching is the translation of learning into appropriate form.*[5] The parent or teacher must do just that, by tailoring environmental tasks to the child's stage of development. There is nothing too difficult about this rule; all it presumes is that the child will not be asked to do anything that he does not have the prerequisite abilities for mastering.[6]

In developing competency, which is a fundamental task of early childhood, *it is important that the child be allowed to assimilate and accommodate to learnings at his own speed.*[7] This includes the extremely important allocation of time for repetition. The child loves repetition, and it is extremely important to his self-concept and self-esteem. Repetition gives the child a chance to savor his successes and make sure the successes are permanently a part of his repertoire of skills. It is the permanency and adequacy of skills that define *competence* or *mastery.*

Evaluation

In terms of evaluation, the key is to be uncritical. The child should be guided from success to success and failure to success with tenderness. He must never be criticized or downgraded for failure. This would be the proverbial "adding insult to injury." The primary objective for evaluation should be to provide the child with the ability to evaluate himself. In psychological terms, this is called "providing him with an internal locus of evaluation,"[8] and there is hardly a more important rule for early childhood learning. The child can be easily made to feel inadequate, for he is extremely sensitive to criticism. It is justifiable to scold the child for misbehavior, but it is never justifiable to scold the child for not achieving competence in a task.

There is now a new notion in education: accountability. This notion proclaims that if the student is unsuccessful, it is the teacher who is at fault. This notion is highly appropriate to early childhood experiences, for *no young child should fail, if the adult has provided him with the necessary prerequisites for each experience.*

The type of evaluation which is imperative to the successfully functioning human being (not just the young child) is self-evaluation. The adult should teach the child, largely through example, the joys and self-fulfillment of striving for excellence, but standards of excellence should not be too rigidly imposed. It is important to teach this with example. Evidence indicates conclusively that the parent or teacher who is constructively self-critical and strives for excellence will produce similar traits in his or her children.[9] The adult who is easily frustrated, frequently finds fault, and is highly critical will not produce children with the ability to be constructively self-evaluative. There is no shortcut for achieving constructive self-criticism.

Montessori has suggested the use of teaching methods, exercises, and toys with built-in capabilities of helping children discover and correct their own errors.[10] This provision for self-correction will enable the child to be self-critical and avoid frustration and external evaluation. There is not enough evidence to show conclusively that this method is effective; but the theory is intuitively pleasing. Certainly, it seems beneficial to limit the possibilities of failure in order to allow for the development of a healthy self-concept. When self-correction is possible, there should be provisions for it. Montessori's own suggestions are most helpful, and the reader is encouraged to peruse her enjoyable and insightful books.

Supportive Adults

The type of adult described above is not rare. Many parents and teachers intuitively know these guidelines and use them frequently. Such adults enjoy exploring with their children, questioning them as equals, and answering their questions, as if each question was potentially the spark of genius. Such adults enjoy contributing information to children and helping them use this information in practical and useful situations. These parents are resourceful and provide the child with interesting challenges, not just sophisticated, commercially produced toys. These adults are encouraging, supportive, and loving. They have empathy for the trials of childhood, and they realize how large the child's tasks are to him. They build him up and tell him how fantastic he is to have accomplished so much. Such adults know intuitively, *and* on the basis of research, what is an appropriate activity for the child at his specific developmental level and what is not. They defer judgment and evaluation on the child's efforts and teach him self-evaluation by example. These parents and teachers are people who are secure in their own accomplishments and are not highly critical of others. Finally, they are people who see in every child the potential for greatness, a potential for which the adult is responsible for nurturing and setting free.

12

Fostering Creativity

Understanding Creativity

Creativity is probably the most controversial and misunderstood notion in education, particularly as it relates to the young child. However, some highly significant strides have been made in recent years. Psychologists and educators are beginning to understand more fully the complex nature of creative expression and the ways in which it can be encouraged. Hardly a parent or teacher would ever dare to criticize creativity as a goal of child development and early educative processes. *Creativity* is a word that is beyond reproach, but it is something that our society has not proved very good at fostering. At home or in the classroom, creativity is frequently viewed as a nuisance and the possessor of the trait is often branded as a "behavior problem." There are tremendous pressures in our society for conformity: encouraging the "correct answer," good behavior, quiet obedience, diligent work, and other such indications that the child is "going well" in the normally prescribed ways.[1] The parent and teacher frequently evaluate a child's performance on the basis of how well behaved she appears to be.

Although I am not recommending the spread of antisocial behavior, I have found that the encouragement of "proper" behavior is often the most serious inhibitor of creativity in young children. J. P. Guilford has coined the term *divergent production* as synonymous with *creativity,* and it is helpful for us to think in these terms.[2] *Divergent production* is behavior which is different, unusual, and free of the constraints of normative evaluation.[3] Divergence, unfortunately, is not something that we have encouraged. We tend to look for the right answer, the proper behavior, and best alternative—or what Guilford calls *convergent production.* Convergent behavior is fine; in fact, many of the exercises presented in this book encourage this type of activity. However, the danger comes when convergence is encouraged to the exclusion of divergence. It is good to be different, and it appears as if our society is beginning to rediscover the importance of individual differences. This is perhaps most evident in ethnic relations; ethnic groups are taking a new pride in their unique heritage. On the individual level, progress in encouraging pride in uniqueness has been much slower. Many of us have had experiences with first impressions. It is natural for human beings to make initial judgments about people. "His behavior sure is poor!" "She looks unpleasant!" These first impressions tend to disrupt our relations with these people and often create a situation where communication breaks down completely. The general assumption in these impressions is that unless people look appealing and act in a normal manner (according to the norms which we ourselves lay down), they are not worth bothering about. This type of thinking does not encourage the realization that there may be richness in diversity.

Without knowing it, many of us stress this very same convergence with our children and students. By prescribing certain behavioral norms, we are consciously, or unconsciously, saying that other behaviors are wrong or undesirable. Adults' unilateral judgments, without thoughtful explanation, can frequently be transferred to children's behaviors. Furthermore, a parent or teacher who restricts a child without explanation can cause the child to seek safety through inactivity and can cause anxiety and fear in the child. In line with this reasoning, it is vitally important that open lines of communication exist between adult and child, even before the child has mastered the ability to communicate verbally herself. Whenever possible, constraints on the child should be minimized by removing or minimizing the chance of unsatisfactory or antisocial behavior. Uniqueness in the child's behavior should be encouraged. "Right" and "wrong" should be eliminated (as much as possible) from the thinking of the parent or teacher, for there is no right or wrong in early childhood exploration and development, especially in the fostering of creativity.

Correlates of Creativity

Many researchers have found the primary correlates of creativity in early childhood education to be venturesomeness, flexibility, independence, playfulness, and originality.[4]

Venturesomeness is an attribute of the child who is permitted to explore things. There is a great deal of research which indicates that venturesomeness and curiosity (which are closely related) will develop naturally by virtue of the child's innate urges to explore.[5] If the child is frequently reprimanded for venturing beyond certain rigidly prescribed environmental limits, she may be severely inhibited in this attribute. The more opportunities that are provided for the child to exhibit and test her natural venturesomeness, the more frequently she will do so in the future. It is up to the parent and teacher to provide the child with appropriate opportunities to behave in this manner, especially in the early stages of development, and to encourage the child in this most important aspect of creative development.

Flexibility is the opposite of rigidity. It is the characteristic of the person who is encouraged to adapt to new situations and develop new behaviors. The child who is flexible can change activities without difficulty, can adapt to environmental changes with little problem, and thrives on novelty and complexity. The child is naturally flexible; therefore, if this characteristic is not exhibited, it is probably because flexibility has not been encouraged. For example, the parent who becomes annoyed when a child constantly switches between toys and appears to have trouble concentrating on one activity will probably inhibit the child's natural flexibility. It is normal for the young child to want to switch activities, and thus a variety of experiences should be made available. In Piagetian terms, the child who is able to accommodate to a wide variety of activities and situations will become the more flexible thinker and doer.[6] The young child has not developed a long attention span, and nothing is gained by forcing her to concentrate longer on one activity than she is capable.

Independence is a characteristic of the creative child that must be treated particularly carefully. It should be understood that close supervision and loving care are compatible with independence. However, supervision can become too strict, and protection can become overbearing. The young child needs to be encouraged to be on her own, to be independent, as much as possible. Exploration of the environment is the first essential step toward achieving independence. The child who is encouraged to explore independently will become more eager for new experience, will develop a more substantial self-concept, and will manifest this independence later on in life. Recent research on achievement motivation has indicated conclusively that independence in childhood is a principal determinant of motivation to achieve in later life.[7] Recently developed training programs in encouraging achievement motivation have stressed independence training as a fundamental training activity.[8]

Forced dependency appears to be among the major causes of conformity and lack of creativity in later life, and it should be avoided with great care.

Playfulness is a trait with which our society has had some difficulty dealing. Certainly, play during playtime is actively encouraged by both parents and teachers. (The nature of play in early learning is discussed in some length elsewhere in this book.) The nature of playfulness, however, transcends conventional ideas of play. *Playfulness* is the ability to play even when not specifically engaged in a conventional activity labeled *play*. The naturally creative child will *playfully* explore, *playfully* combine objects, *playfully* try out new motor skills, *playfully* attempt to extend the limits of her known environment, and even *playfully* misbehave. When possible these playful adventures should be encouraged. Play is much more than games and toys; it is a way of acting and thinking that challenges convention, restriction, and the usual.[9] In fact, Einstein and other extraordinary creative geniuses described their own acts of creation and invention as play.[10] To compartmentalize our activities into categories of *work* and *play* is a powerful force inhibiting creative expression. It is the merging of such activities that we conventionally refer to as work and play that tends to foster constructive creativity and personal imagination.

Originality is a term that is frequently misunderstood, but it is a term that is at the very basis of creativity. Originality does not mean the invention of something that has never existed before; it more frequently describes the discovery, or rediscovery, of something that has existed for some time. For the young child, everything is new and different; to her originality means the trying of new things, discovering of new combinations, experimenting with new objects, and discovering of new relationships. The individual who is rewarded for originality in her early experience will be much more likely to make more original contributions later in life.

Through the encouragement of venturesomeness, flexibility, independence, playfulness, and originality, the young child learns that there is not only one answer to a question. She learns to have confidence and pride in her normal urge to explore, her curiosity, her experimentation, and her inquisitiveness. The parent and teacher who encourages creativity will probably be required to work harder, be more vigilant, and exercise more restraint; but, in the long-run, these efforts will produce a happier, better-adjusted, and more creative person. There is considerable evidence to indicate that the child who has been taught to rigidly control her own behavior, take care not to disturb things, and always seek the correct way of doing things will continue to seek the conventional way of doing things throughout life.[11]

Creativity in Learning

In all learning there is a "curriculum" or plan, either explicit or implied. The recommended activities in this book can be viewed as being a curriculum for learning basic concepts. However, a curriculum should never be invariant and rigid. It should change with the child's needs and the desire of every child to express herself creatively. In essence, creativity in learning means going beyond the curriculum and expressing something very personal and individualistic. In this sense, creativity is the very basis of humanness. Too often educational experiences are so rigidly defined that there is little leeway for personal expression. In early learning, it is vitally important that the child be given the opportunity to express herself divergently as well as convergently. In adults, this need to express one's individuality and uniqueness often becomes repressed and obscured by habit and the demands of everyday living. However, creative self-expression is a significant aspect of a child's growth process, in terms of both intellectual and personality development. It is one of the hypotheses of the current treatment of concept formation that the very act of creating categories of experience is inherently creative.[12] Opportunities for creativity should extend even beyond the natural limits of activities. Creative self-expression should be encouraged at all times, in all ways. When children see that their creativity is valued, they will tend to display it more and more. Remember, though, that it is unwise and difficult to evaluate creative expression in normal qualitative terms of "good" and "bad." Creativity should transcend these ultimately limiting labels.

Processes of Creativity

Perhaps the greatest mistake that can be made in adult reaction to early creative activity is viewing only the result of the creative act. The most important part of creation for the child (and that is what counts most) is the *process* itself. The product is secondary until much later in the child's development. The *process* of scribbling, the *process* of painting, the *process* of arranging things, these are the truly meaningful aspects of early creativity. Unfortunately our society is dependent upon products. Students in school are infrequently evaluated on the process of learning because it is only the final result that seems to matter. In early childhood learning, especially in the home, this should certainly not be the case. Young children love the feeling of causing things to happen; this is the feeling of "effectance."[13] Leaving the child to her own devices, supplying a rich environment (full of processes), providing unobtrusive supervision, and giving continual encouragement combine to become a very effective strategy for fostering creativity in early childhood.

Too often we tend to inflict our own ideas upon young children and decide for them what they want to do. Too often we correct them, employing adult standards. We tend to show children how something (for example, a toy) is supposed to work. We buy children elaborate toys and games. We give them coloring books with predetermined lines. Instead, we should let them experiment, not to please us, but to please themselves. If children make a mess or if the products of their efforts are not too pretty, who cares? If they have gotten pleasure from the activity, then it has been worthwhile. There is too much in our society that breeds conformity; we should try to make learning and play as creative as possible for young children.

Drawing and Painting

There is hardly a better way for the child to express herself, and learn in the process, than through drawing and painting. These are activities that the young child can actively engage in, certainly by the age of two and frequently much earlier. The idea is not to have the child produce a work of art, a monumental masterpiece, but for her to have fun and be able to express herself and her individuality. This is the greatest gift you can give the very young child—herself. From the most awkward and elemental scribbles great things tend to grow.[14]

Kinesthetic experience (involving movement of the body) is also an essential part of early development.[15] From early infancy, the child is actively participating in experiments with body movements: reaching, changing position, touching. The satisfaction that results from successful kinesthetic experience is unrivaled by any other early satisfaction or pleasure. Scribbling and then drawing are extensions of this very fundamental pleasure. In early childhood, after all, the body is the most substantial part of the child's existence. The child who engages in relatively uncontrolled scribbling is enjoying what she is doing and should not be encouraged to move on to more representational drawing. According to Viktor Lowenfeld, such uncontrolled scribbling marks an important milestone in child development and also indicates that the child is just not ready for more controlled kinesthetic activity.[16] This is also indicative of the fact that the child is not yet ready for other controlled motor activities such as eating, dressing, etc. Lowenfeld has shown that it is "both senseless and harmful to teach activities requiring proper motor coordination" before the child is ready for such activity.[17] Lowenfeld is also the severest of critics of overly structured activities in early childhood, such as coloring books, viewing them as inhibitors of creativity.[18]

We should also recognize the difference between art for communication and art for self-expression. As Di Leo says, "In contrast to the adult who is writing to communicate, the scribbler does not seem to be trying to tell *us* anything" [emphasis added].[19] We are the ones who try to see meaning in their playful expressions. It is the hang-up of the adult that everything has to have *objective meaning*. Ultimately, it is motor control and mastery of the body that the young child aims at achieving in these early months and years. All her enjoyment is derived from kinesthetic sensation, emerging competence, and explorations of these new abilities and feelings. Repetition is part of the child's need for mastery, and repeating the same scribbles should not be viewed as conflicting with creativity. It is part of the very same process.

Later, the thrill of motor control gives way to other excitements, such as experimentation with color. For the young child, form is not nearly as important as motor activity.[20] However, an interest in shape and form develops in its proper sequence, at its proper time. Scribbling is an important developmental step that will help lead the child to better motor coordination, improved visual acuity, and eventually more representational art.

Various materials are suggested for these early creative experiences. Finger paints and felt markers (water soluble) are most appropriate. Pencils are not recommended because of the ease with which their sharp point might break; water colors tend to run into each other and prevent the development of discrete lines, directly under the child's control. Lowenfeld suggests that even the use of different colors in the early stages of scribbling can be distracting to the child, because she may spend time searching for the proper color which can interrupt the fluid motions of her arm. Lowenfeld recommends that colors be used when the child is ready to name her scribbles.[21]

Clay is very effective at this level. Clay allows the child to create a unique shape or form with a minimum of effort. Clay is also a type of material which affords the child a sense of mastery and competence. The act of molding is a tremendously significant one. It permits the child to use many of her muscles, which might not be used in scribbling, and increase other aspects of her perceptual and motor coordination.

Any type of manipulative activity will probably help to stimulate the young child's creative urges. In addition to paints and clay, blocks and sand are superb stimuli for creative growth. Building things with blocks, or just arranging them, can be an important creative outlet. When you think of the hundreds, even thousands, of different arrangements or patterns that can be formed, you will have some appreciation for the creative potential that is inherent in most every early childhood activity. The only guideline to remember is that the materials should be appropriate for the child's level of perceptual-motor development. The materials should be large enough to be grasped and handled with relative ease, but not so large that materials become awkward to handle. *Appropriateness* is the important watchword.

Gradually, the child will begin to develop an interest in representation, but there is no rush for this to occur. This may begin to occur at or around the age of three. Scribblers may discover, on their own, that some of their scribbles resemble things in their environment. A circle might appear to resemble a person's head, and then the child may proceed to draw a face in it. A square might appear to resemble a house, and a triangular roof might soon follow. It is important that the child make these discoveries independently. For some children, representational art may come later; there is no relationship between the age of the emergence of representational art and intelligence or creativity. Most children develop normally at their own pace, given the proper encouragement, enriched environment, and facilities.

The most important thing to remember about the emergence of representational art is that the adult should never ask, "What is that?" According to Di Leo, when such a question is asked, the child will feel obliged to play the game, supplying a title that might inhibit her natural progress.[22] There is no reason to rush objectivity; the subjective experience is important as well. The most important thing is to free the child from any external constraints on her creativity and self-expression. When the child is ready to discuss the nature of her efforts, she will undoubtedly do so. Until then, we should leave the child alone to experiment with as many creative art forms as possible and help her by celebrating the joy of creativity.

Another guideline for the adult in guiding young children's art is that "copying" should never be encouraged. If the child wants to copy something on his own terms, then fine. But never ask children to copy a picture; this may limit their creativity. As Di Leo explains, the important thing is to get the child to express what is inside of her as much as possible.[23]

The development of representational art will come in leaps and strides. As language develops, the child will begin to explain his drawings and other art work and tell stories about them. Since there is a tremendous early fascination with the human face and body, this subject matter will probably serve as the basis of early representational drawing. There will also be other objects in the pictures, but most often there is little relationship between the person and the objects. It is recommended that parents and teachers keep a file of the child's art work because it will be most fascinating to compare early and later work. This will be a good indication of the natural stages of creative growth and perceptual-motor development. There is, however, no reason to evaluate it. The adult who listens carefully, discusses with the child intelligently, and encourages artistic endeavor will certainly stimulate the child's innate creativity and desire for self-expression. Creative development takes time and support, but the effort will produce enduring effects on the child's ability to cope with her environment spontaneously, competently, and creatively.

Stimulating Creative Ideas

It should be remembered that in early childhood just about everything is a "creative" activity (in the broadest sense of the word). Play is creative; painting is creative; scribbling is creative; molding clay is creative; language development is creative; body movement is creative. The widening world of the young child is one creative discovery after another. Early childhood is a celebration of creativity. But there is probably nothing more creative than the *ideas* of the young child. These ideas are fresh and unspoiled. They are new and oftentimes illogical (by adult standards). They are unconstrained by the boundaries and practicalities of adult thinking. In short, they are wonderful.[24]

The best way to stimulate children's creative thought processes is to continually ask questions and comment upon events and parts of the environment. "What do you think of that?" "How do you feel about this?" Not only do questions like these ultimately stimulate children to think on their own and give their own ideas, but it is also good for their self-concepts. By doing this, you are saying, "Your opinions are important; they really matter." When talking to children, it is important not to put *your* words in their mouths. It is also important to honestly express the way you feel. This is just good communication, and good communication is part of the process of fostering creativity.

Young children have wonderful ideas about the way things work. When your child asks you a question, don't just tell her the answer. Work with her to find the answer; stimulate the child to think about phenomena and processes. Bruner has indicated that good education is the process of rediscovery.[25] All children can't be expected to be Albert Einsteins or Johann Sebastian Bachs, but all children can rediscover things. It is so much more meaningful when the child finds out things independently. "Where does electricity come from?" "What makes the car run?" "Where does the sound in the radio come from?" The world is full of questions, and every child is full of potential answers. It is so much easier to give the answers yourself, but this makes the important question-and-answer process a relatively passive one for the child, and it greatly diminishes the potential for creative development.

The definition of *creativity* is fundamentally different in early childhood than it is later in life. The young child is creative at all times, when given the chance. Once children start taking tests and are compared with other youngsters in their age group, creativity becomes more of an exclusive club. This is unfortunate because it tends to exclude those who are relatively creative (compared with their own creative potential). Because formal schooling tends to be so evaluative an experience, these distinctions and comparisons can have a devastating effect upon children's future creative development. This is why it is so very important that creativity be fostered in early childhood. Creativity tends to take a back seat to measures of "intelligence" and "achievement."[26] In later years, these measures really seem to be the only ones that count. Possibly because creativity is such an ill-defined trait.

Much of what we do know about creativity can be attributed to the work of Guilford,[27] Getzels and Jackson,[28] and Wallach and Kogan.[29] These researchers have studied the issue rather carefully and have fundamentally determined that there is little correlation (or relationship) between creativity and intelligence. This finding, which is a rather general one, has caused monumental problems in the fostering of creativity in later childhood and adulthood. After all, schools exist basically to teach intellectual (cognitive) skills, and largely in groups. Creativity is a trait that is not directly linked to cognitive skills and is best nurtured on an individual basis.

This chapter emphasizes the critical importance of the encouragement of creativity early in life. If it does not come during these first few years, it might not be developed at all. As society becomes more and more technologically oriented, it becomes harder and harder to nurture the uniqueness of each individual and see clearly the contribution that each individual has to make. Early childhood is the ideal time.

Motivation and Early Learning

Motivation is the field of psychology which attempts to explain human behavior. Through studies in the psychology of motivation we have come to better understand why people do what they do. We constantly hear the term *motivation* used ("He sure is *motivated* in school" or "I just wish I were *motivated* to do that"), but what does the term really mean and what is its significance for early learning?

Motivation used to be accounted for by basic needs. It was observed that animals and humans behave when they have to do so; when they are hungry, thirsty, tired, frightened, insecure, etc. They are *driven* to act by needs, both innate and learned. According to this view, all behavior is caused by a biological imperative or a deficiency.[1] This view of motivation proved to be quite satisfactory to explain the observed behavior of laboratory animals, such as rats and rabbits; yet it did not prove quite so helpful in explaining more complex forms of human behavior. It was found that certain human behaviors could not be so easily accounted for in these simple motivational terms. The behavior of young children, for example, baffled many observers. Children tend to explore and exhibit intense curiosity, not because of a biological need, but because they are inherently curious. The research of Hebb,[2] Berlyne,[3] and White,[4] has significantly contributed to a much broader appreciation of the complexity of human motivation.

Intrinsic and Extrinsic Motivation

It has been quite recently discovered that there are both intrinsic as well as extrinsic motivations. *Extrinsic* motivation is largely a function of need.

When people are motivated by desire for money, need for food, need for security, need for affection, and other such drives, they are viewed as being *extrinsically* motivated. When people do something just for the pleasure of doing it, the activity is viewed as *intrinsically* motivating. Obviously, both types of motivation are important in understanding and appreciating human behavior.[5]

Perhaps the most striking discovery of recent years in motivational psychology has been that people tend to attempt to attain an "optimal level of arousal," or the level of motivation that is right for each individual.[6] This contrasts with the once-popular view that people always try to reduce their level of motivation through the satisfaction of needs. This new notion holds that these "motivated states" can be pleasant and are actively sought by the individual. Maslow has contrasted these two views of motivation, calling them "deficiency motivation" and "growth motivation," respectively.[7] The important point is that humans do not always act in order to reduce their arousal, but they frequently act to increase it. Researchers have pointed to man's apparent need for excitement to support this notion. We tend to flock to suspense movies and read books which are carefully designed to lead us to levels of emotional intensity. The optimal level of arousal tends to differ considerably from person to person, but for each individual this level is vitally important for understanding behavior. We do not behave only to reduce our hunger or thirst or to satisfy other primary biological drives. We also behave in ways that will make our lives more exciting, even if that excitement frequently comes only from secondhand sources (vicarious experiences), like films and books.

The young child is in a more enviable position in terms of growth motivation. For him, excitement is at the very heart of every activity and exploration undertaken. Everything is new; everything is exciting; most everything is intrinsically motivating. The young child explores his environment naturally because he is curious, not as a result of external rewards. Exploration is at the very basis of early childhood experience. Given an appropriate environment, rich in lessons and safe to explore, children will express their natural curiosity in wondrous and novel ways.

Most early childhood learning occurs because the child *wants* to learn, not because of the lure of external reward. This is what makes early childhood learning such a rewarding process for all concerned. What is it that changes the pattern of learning from intrinsic to extrinsic? Why is it that older learners need specific inducements to learn, while young children tend to learn for the sheer joy of it? These are among the fundamental questions of educational psychology; the answer would solve many of our current educational problems. They are questions that are currently under study by this author and many other researchers.

Young children are avid learners; they want to explore; they want to create; they want to make things; they want to find answers. The best way to keep this intrinsic motivation active as long as possible is to react appropriately to it. Tasks must be appropriate to the child's level of development and as interesting as possible for him. The essential lesson from research is to make the task as attractive as possible and not have to "bribe" the child to do things.[8] These bribes, or external inducements, may tend to obscure the intrinsic attractiveness of learning, exploring, and discovering new knowledge. In fact, researchers have found that monetary rewards and academic grades tend to replace intrinsic motivation with extrinsic motivation.[9] Intrinsic motivation should be fostered whenever possible. The rule of thumb to remember is to provide the child with enough time for each activity so that he can master it at his own pace. Children also like to repeat tasks that they have already mastered. However, be aware of when the child might be losing his enthusiasm for a certain task and give him something else to do. The provision for rich and varied resources in the child's environment should do the trick.

Motives, Expectancies, and Incentives

In very simple terms, motivation appears to be the result of three interacting factors: motives, expectancies, and incentives. *Motives* are dispositions of the individual that, when aroused, may cause him to behave in a certain way. There are many differing opinions about the nature of human motives. Murray has described the following basic human motives: achievement, affiliation (need for other people), autonomy, aggression, understanding, dominance, superiority, and harm-avoidance (avoiding pain).[10] In addition to these motives, White added competence,[11] Hill added activity,[12] and Hebb[13] and Berlyne[14] have described an exploration motive. These last three motives are particularly significant for the young child, who seeks a high level of activity, seeks competence, and enjoys exploring his environment wherever and whenever possible. Motives like these exist in most everyone to varying degrees, and the motive composition of a person is a measure of his individuality. Some motives are innate and others are learned through experience.

What determines whether a motive is aroused or not? The answer appears to lie in a combination of expectancies and incentives. *Expectancies* are representative of what a person thinks will occur in a certain situation. Psychologists have found this to be a vital aspect of human behavior. One significant theory holds that when the world is too predictable, people will become bored, and probably will not behave with much intensity.[15] However, when the world is surprising, and unpredict-able, people tend to be stimulated and behave with considerable vigor. This is the reason why very young children tend to be so active. Their world has not yet become predictable; everything is still exciting, new, and different. The best way to keep this extraordinary activity level high is to make certain that the young child's stimulation never becomes *too* predictable. Certainly, young children need some measure of predictabil-ity and security, but not as much as the average adult. The young child thrives on newness and stimulation.[16] And novelty is a very important part of the nature of motivation in early childhood.

Incentives form a very controversial part of motivation. If the task is exciting in itself, then no additional incentives may be necessary. How-ever, if a task is boring and tedious, the motivator might well have to add *external incentives* to the task situation. Unfortunately, human activity is not always pleasurable in itself. Learning, too, can be difficult, tedious, and boring. The job of a successful motivator is to design a learning situation in such a way that its pleasurable aspects are emphasized. The essential task of the successful motivator is to make learning activities enjoyable and interesting for the learner. This is easy to say, but it is more difficult to do. However, much of this book aims at making this job a little easier. Interestingly, making a task easy does not seem to necessarily make it attractive. Many people need the challenge of a difficult task. Researchers have found that people with high achievement motivation tend to prefer tasks at which they will fail from time to time.[17] Otherwise, such people tend to get bored. Motivation requires arousal, and arousal comes from excitement, difficulty, risk, complexity, and many other factors.

The best way to find out if the child is being appropriately motivated is simply to observe carefully. It does not take much observational ability to determine when a child is aroused and when he is bored. Don't let a child persist at activities which are too easy for him, but don't let him become frustrated by activities which are too difficult. Look for activities which are challenging, but not overwhelming. When you find activities that really stimulate the child, try to invent new forms of that activity.

Summary

Reviewing the nature of motivation as discussed here, we can be rela-tively certain that an activity is motivating for the child when appropriate motives are aroused by expectancies and incentives. We know that all young children are natural learners, at least when they are placed in an appropriate environment for learning. Young children exhibit strong motives for exploration, curiosity, activity, competence, mastery, and knowledge seeking. In order to arouse these motives, it is important to place the child in a situation that will be challenging, perhaps a situation in which he does not know quite what to expect. When appropriately selected, most early childhood learning activities and exploratory situations are intrinsically motivating, with incentives which are part of the task.

14

Summary

The young child is a remarkable learner, the kind of motivated student that any teacher would be proud to teach. She has a tremendous thirst for knowledge and experience, thrives on challenge, and is excited by almost everything. The world of the young child is one wonder after another. The preceding chapters have attempted to develop a context in which these remarkable feats can be viewed. It is during these early years of life that the young child is laying the foundation for all future learning and the interpretation of subsequent experience.

In summary, Part 1 is an integration of a vast amount of existing research. I have endeavored to provide a basis for understanding the most significant intellectual development in early childhood, the formation of basic concepts which will serve to organize future experience. In essence, this book is based on the following generalizations culled from research and theoretical findings. They bear repeating here:

1. Early experience is essential to intellectual, perceptual, and motor development.
2. Most children cannot and should not develop beyond their stage of readiness, but within each stage great variance is possible.
3. Perceptual-based and sensory learning is the foundation upon which most future learning will build.
4. Perceptual and motor learning which does not develop fully in early childhood may never properly develop.

5. A large portion of the intellectual capabilities of children is determined by the age of five.

6. Early learning is a direct function of the quantity and quality of experience.

7. Successful interaction with the environment causes the young child to desire more such contacts, thus increasing the overall level of experience attained.

8. Independent learning is pleasurable learning.

9. Learning experiences which are most appropriate to the child's level of development will be the most rewarding.

10. Independence breeds creativity, autonomy, and feelings of competence.

11. Concepts are the foundation of all thought.

12. Concepts serve to organize experience and render it into usable form for subsequent experience.

13. The quality of future experience is largely a function of how well previous experience has been organized and stored.

14. Cooperative educational experience, between adult and child, is the most effective form of early education.

15. Children, especially very young children, tend to be attracted to novelty, complexity, and challenge.

16. All learning is based on a foundation of previous learning; it is hierarchical.

17. Early education can and should be an ecstatic enterprise for both adults and children.

18. Too many of the resources of early education go unused and wasted; many of these are simple household items.

19. Early education is really a very simple, commonsense enterprise.

20. It is never too early for educational experiences to start; we should never underestimate the ability of young children to learn through experience and their own activity.

The years of early childhood are the most exciting in life. It is unfortunate that so few of us remember these wondrous years of excitement and novelty. We should relive these years vicariously with our children and share in their early experience and wonderment. It will help us experience our adult world with a little more freshness and exhilaration. The wonderful years of early childhood are times to be shared. They are the young child's gift to us.

part 2

ACTIVITIES

Introduction

The activities suggested in this part are intended for just that purpose: to *suggest* creative opportunities for early childhood enrichment and education. There are millions of possible activities which can excite and stimulate the young child. The following are but a few suggestions that have proven to be successful in the past. It is hoped that they will stimulate your imagination and help you design your own activities and materials to supplement those presented here. This compilation is not intended to be exhaustive; it is just a beginning. There are no strict "rules" governing the appropriateness of the activities to the child's readiness or level of development. Each activity is presented in such a way as to give guidance to the reader, but not to specify in any detail the instructions or procedures. It is hoped that these activities, presented as they are, will provide the adult and child with an important opportunity to explore the environment together with some structure and organization. It is vital to note that these activities are intended only to supplement the normal explorations of the young child, discussed at length in Part 1. There is no substitute for independent exploration which is such a vital part of the early experience of any young child.

The great teacher of young children is the adult who provides a rich, yet organized, environment for children to explore. This is particularly true during these first early years. Exploration is the key to early childhood learning, and more structured experiences should not get in the way of this necessary outlet for normal curiosity. It is up to the adult to decide when to use these activities and when to let the child explore independently. Ideally, there should be a mix between these two approaches. Early childhood education at its best is a cooperative enterprise between adult and child, with mutual respect and understanding. The following activities have been carefully selected to enrich this cooperative learning experience. They have also been designed and selected for their consistency with existing research and experiential evidence on the intellectual, kinesthetic, social, and perceptual needs of young children. It is hoped that Part 1 has provided the reader with an adequate background for appreciating and using these activities.

The world is an exciting place for young children. However, to a great extent, children need the adult to bring this environment to them. There are many resources well within their reach, but there are also many things which must be pointed out and presented to them. You should be aware of the limits of the child's exploratory ability and recognize those resources that are readily available to him and those that are outside his limits.

The items and objects suggested in the pages that follow are just a beginning of the list of significant educational resources. A box of toothpicks can become a valuable educational resource in imaginative hands, as can a seashell, a stone, some rubber bands, and some wooden spools. *There is probably no more creative experience than the designing of activities for, and using them with, young children.* These activities should stress creativity, experimentation, manipulation, movement, and other vital needs of the young child.

The activities following are aimed primarily at the important *concrete concepts* which were discussed at length in Part 1. These are the concepts that children learn through their sensory explorations and active manipulations when exploring the things in their environment. The principal emphasis should be on giving young children firsthand experience, experience with real things in all their profusion and variety. The world is a vast *feast* for the young child, of which these activities are just the *appetizer*. Don't starve the child of experience.

Please view these activities in their proper perspective. They are ideas upon which there are hundreds of variations. The parent or teacher is the best judge of the specifics of each activity, and the best judge of the readiness of the child for the activity being considered. There is no substitute for the unique qualifications of both parent and teacher for providing the young child with the support, attention, and advice that are needed to implement any early childhood activity or enrichment program.

There is no reason why every child should not have every advantage that can be given to him. These are advantages based on all we know from research about early education, the unique abilities and creativity of every parent, and an environment which is rich in materials, human resources, and activities. This book is advocating a position calling for the provision of equal early educational opportunity for every child to do what he does best and does naturally. What the young child does best is explore. By providing him with the materials and organization for such exploring, along with concerned and knowledgable adult guidance, the child will do the rest. Intellectual growth is a natural process, but it requires certain richness within the educational environment.

There are, however, a few practical suggestions that might be offered for assuring that the activities that you use and design are most appropriately presented to the child and most adaptable to his unique needs. These suggestions include the following:

1. *Begin with simple activities that are well within the child's ability.* The important and enduring lesson of early childhood is personal competence. If the child feels competent early in life, he will transfer this self-confidence to all future endeavors.

2. *Let the child explore and experiment as much as he likes.* Do not force him to go on to another activity before he is ready to do so. To encourage exploration and self-expression is to tell the child that his ideas are worthy of being tried. There is no rush for intellectual progress; consolidation and mastery of learning are the important factors, not speed of completion.

3. *Allow the child to practice the same skills over and over again, if he wishes, and most children do.* Repetition and practice are two of the most important notions in early childhood learning. They allow the child to gain complete mastery over skills, as well as to think and reflect upon the ideas that lie behind the skills being mastered.

4. *Introduce activities in a relaxed context; do not lose sight of the fact that learning should be fun.* The activities suggested in this book are really games. In such activities, play and learning should become one and the same: this is a characteristic of truly great education. Learning will become a joy.

5. *If the child becomes restless and tired, do not continue with the activity.* If you force the child to learn, he will soon become resistant to it. It cannot be overemphasized how important it is to equate learning with pleasure in these early educational endeavors.

6. *If the child does not seem to enjoy an activity move right on to something else.* It is only natural that children will enjoy some activities more than others. There are also many other factors that

might affect the child's attitudes toward certain activities including disposition, readiness for the activity, and the way it has been presented.

7. *Be aware of signs that might indicate if the child is having problems with certain activities: be diagnostic.* Look for the signs of boredom, impatience, dissatisfaction, nervousness, lack of comprehension, inattention, lack of preparedness, perceptual problems, or other signs which might tell you that there is a need for reassessing what you or the child is doing. This diagnostic ability can be easily developed in time, if you allow yourself to view the learning situation objectively.

8. *If you discover the possibility of any major learning disabilities in your child or if you find that the child is consistently inattentive, bored, tired, or unable to perceive certain things, consult your pediatrician.* Sometimes there are perceptual difficulties which are caused by physical problems. There may be nothing wrong, but it is always better to be safe than sorry.

9. *Go slowly with the activities; there is no need to do everything at once.* Gradual learning is stressed in most activities, and it will probably be the most enduring learning. You will learn just how much stimulation the child can take and when he has had too much.

10. *Be as spontaneous as possible in organizing the activities.* You do not have to specify a particular place and time for everything. The more spontaneous and relaxed an activity's context, the more fun and enjoyable it will probably be for the child. Ritual learning sometimes becomes forced and artificial.

11. *Keep track of the child's progress by jotting down occasional observations.* These notes will provide you with an invaluable record of the child's growth, a way to organize activities in a more systematic manner, a means for discovering trends in the child's development that might be helpful, or simply for learning more about your child and yourself.

12. *Take advantage of as many of the lessons as possible related to use of activities, build on them, talk about them, and use them as jumping off points for other lessons.* The more of your own creativity that you integrate into the suggested activities, the more meaningful they will be for your child.

13. *Talk to your child about everything.* There is no need to drill your child in language use; exposure to language is quite sufficient.

14. *Always be aware of new developments in early childhood educa-tion.* Expose yourself to as many different ideas on child develop-ment as possible. You are ultimately the major force in the child's life, and much of his future success in school and in life will be determined by the richness of his first few years.

15. *Remember that whatever your child learns from these activities and other preschool enrichment programs is a bonus which will serve him well for his entire lifetime.* In a real sense, this is an extremely significant investment in his future, perhaps the most important one you can make.

16. *Cooperative educational activities between adult and child can become the most meaningful part of the lives of all concerned.* There is no greater fulfillment than sharing knowledge and grow-ing together. Many parents and teachers are too often passive observers of children's development. This book aims at making the adult the prime mover in the intellectual growth process, the most exciting process there is in all the world!

17. *Finally, remember that the home is a magnificent educational institution, with almost unlimited built-in possibilities for ex-panding the horizons of children.* Use every opportunity you can to point out new learnings. Explore the shapes, colors, textures, functions, and other attributes of the multitude of objects around the house. There is no reason why every day cannot be meaningful for early childhood education.

First Year Materials

Colorful cubes   Sugar cubes
Suspended rings   Cup
Mobiles   Patterned designs
Small ball   Suspended figures
Rattles   Rubber squeaking toys
Sound cubes   Rubber blocks
Spoon   Water toys
Mirror   Clothespins
String   Basket
Cloth, for decorating and hiding   Scooper
Bells, dinner and wrist

The newborn infant requires constant attention for stimulation. Every experience must be brought to the child, but stimulation need not be elaborate. The most important stimulation during the first three months of life is the proximity of an adult because the newborn is fascinated by just looking at the human face, hearing sounds, and having frequent body contact.

During the first year of life, the infant's activities are limited by his relative difficulty to explore independently and to manipulate objects and by his lack of locomotor abilities. Perhaps the most important stimulation for the infant during this time is what the adult does instinctively. Body contact between infant and adult is extremely important. Such a simple operation as getting the child to grasp another's finger is an activity of potentially great significance. It helps to develop the infant's recognition of aspects of the outside world, the differentiation of self and others, visual ability, hand-eye coordination, manual dexterity, and general motor skills. There is really no need for elaborate activities during this first year because *everything* is new to the infant. Attention getting, attention focusing, reaching, grasping, and basic sensory stimulation comprise the most important emphasis for the first year of life. Almost all the stimulation the child receives during this period has to be brought to him. The resulting adult responsibility is enormous. The first year of life is most exciting, as the child begins to come to grips with his world and the people and objects in it. The following activities seek to foster the development of the basic sensorimotor intelligence that Piaget has described, as the infant learns to adapt to the novel stimuli around him. Learning by assimilating new information and accommodating to new experiences, the infant is already an astute learner. The following activities stress joyous learning, a partnership between adult and child. The most basic activities in this section can certainly begin by the third or fourth week. Beyond that guideline, there are few predetermined patterns of behavior. Your own assessment of the infant's readiness will be your best guide. The division of the first year into two sections suggesting activities for infants three weeks to five months and activities for infants five months to one year is only to provide some direction and not to be thought as a rigid division.

Activities:
Three Weeks to
Five Months

Dangling Objects

The newborn infant is not yet able to see faraway objects; her vision is limited to people and objects within a few feet of her. The very young child is fascinated with form and color, and it is recommended that colorful and complex objects be presented to the infant for visual stimulation. Dangling objects, suspended above the infant's crib, permit the child to fixate her eyes on objects when the parent is not present and develop her all-important visual abilities. Furthermore, researchers have found that infants prefer complex objects to simple ones.

Suspended objects are the ideal stimuli for the young infant. Most adults cannot spend all their time constructing novel situations for their children, and the suspended object is the ideal answer to the problem. Such objects provide the infant with an almost unlimited combination of visual stimulation, at least for a while. Constantly moving, changing direction, altering orientation, and changing position relative to the background, suspended objects can contribute significantly toward the creation of a rather large foundation of early visual experience.

Dangling objects can be constructed from almost any material as long as the colors are bright and the objects can move. This might be due to the relative complexity of the human face as a visual object, the first stimulus the newborn fixates her eyes upon. Motion can make a relatively simple object like a dangling ring into a fascinating stimulus. The ring is a good object to familiarize the child with because, later, the ring will prove to be an important item for grasping and manual manipulation. The adult can also construct mobiles of varied colors and shapes to hang above the infant's crib for further variety of visual experience.

Types of objects which can be suspended above the child's crib are virtually unlimited. The only guidelines are that the objects be large enough to be seen clearly, with a variety of shapes and colors, and be attractive when in motion. Some objects, besides rings, that might prove satisfactory suspended stimuli are dolls, cardboard cutouts, colored string, toy animals, spoons, balls of multi-colored yarn, and patterned forms.

A new dimension can be added to the exercise by suspending objects which have different textures, different patterns of movement, and different sounds. The dangling of objects which make noise can be of real value, especially when the child is able to manipulate the objects and cause the sounds herself. The infant will get great satisfaction from being the cause of some event, whether it be moving an object or making it "talk." Particularly appropriate in this context might be a colorful box filled with different noise-making objects, a toy that emits squeaks when touched or squeezed, dangling bells, or simply a dinner bell.

Another important consideration is the need for suspended objects which will be appropriate for multi-sensory exploration: putting into her mouth, touching with her body, listening to, and caressing. The more objects available that provide the infant with multiple sensations, the better she will learn to recognize the different properties of things, the greater will be her familiarity with the things that make up her environment, and the more experience her concepts will be based upon.

The Suspended Ring

Experts on infant behavior have found that a colorful rubber ring, suspended above the infant's crib, is a particularly useful stimulus during
the early months of life. At first, the ring serves only as a visual target
providing the child an opportunity to attend to a moving object. The
movement can be made increasingly complex: at first moving side to side,
then back and forth, and finally in circles. The importance of this type of
stimulation has been shown time and time again to be considerable,
especially for the development of the visual perceptual abilities that form
the basic element of most future environmental exploration.

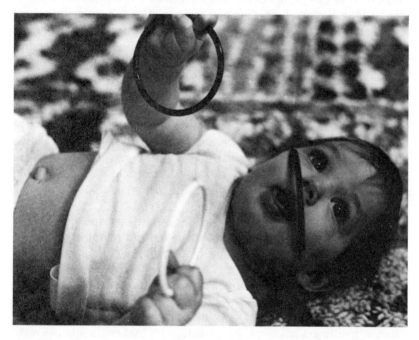

As soon as the child is able to lift her arms above her head, she is
ready to begin touching the suspended ring and moving it herself. This
behavior contributes to the facilitation of visual and motor coordination.
In addition, it provides the infant with an opportunity to manipulate her
environment independently. The newborn's environment is initially so
limited that this small, manipulative opportunity is extremely significant.
The suspended ring is an example of just how, in early infancy, a very
simple activity can have far-reaching developmental effects.

Although it is not important what type of ring is used, it is recommended that some variety be introduced into the activity. Different
colored or patterned rings can be substituted from time to time. Also, it is

good practice to occasionally move the ring differently and present it at different heights.

Grasping Suspended Objects

Initially, the infant is able only to view objects and follow them with her eyes. Soon, she will become able to grasp and obtain them. The process of developing the ability to obtain a desired object is an important early infant development and represents the integration of a number of perceptual and motor abilities. It is the beginning of a substantial degree of early autonomy. This development is significantly related to the infant's ability to discriminate between her own body and external stimuli, her recognition of objects located in space, and the improvement of eye-hand coordination.

Suspended objects, such as the rubber ring, can be placed within the child's reach while being held by the adult or by being attached to some sort of elastic material. Perhaps, initially, the object should be handheld in order to judge the most appropriate distance above the child. The activity should be challenging, but not too difficult.

The advantage of the ring for such activities is that it can be so easily grasped in many different places, using a uniform grasping procedure. In addition, the ring is large and colorful enough to attract the child's attention. The ring is also relatively light, has interesting movement patterns, and is a very flexible item for other follow-up activities.

Spatial Learning

The use of suspended and dangling objects is also extremely important for the early development of a concept of space. The child must learn many of the perceptual abilities that adults take for granted. One of these perceptual abilities is the perception of space. Suspended objects and the infant's visual and motor activities in apprehending them provide invaluable experience with spatial relationships. Infants without the stimulation of crib adornments may not learn as quickly or as fully about such things as the perception of depth, the ability to distinguish between figure and background, and the ability to follow objects through space. These early perceptual learnings come quite naturally, but they must develop through direct experience with objects and activities which provide the raw material for such learning. Objects which move through space are fundamental facilitators of this important learning.

The infant's crib is really quite a barren environment, unless it is adorned in some way. The addition of mobiles increases the experience of the infant in so many different ways. Through the development of reaching, grasping, and exploratory responses, the infant is able to inquire into the nature of space, realizing that an object in the foreground is not part of the background and that space is arranged in depth. In the early months of life, the visual, attentional, reaching, and grasping responses are a fundamental part of the perceptual learning and integration that is so important to all subsequent early childhood learning tasks.

A new dimension in spatial learning is achieved when the child is able to view the world in a sitting position. From this point on, the infant is more able to participate in some semi-structured learning activities, which provide the child with a greater insight into her relationship to objects, other people, and the outside world.

Patterned Designs

Researchers have found that decorating the child's crib with cloth of varied colors and patterns provides the infant with a further dimension of visual stimulation. In addition to the valuable mobile stimulation of dangling objects, such hangings provide stable stimulation of colors and patterns, bright and attention getting. The young infant loves to look at interesting colors and patterns, and the availability of substantial opportunities for visual experience will provide him additional stimulation.

Later, when the infant achieves a certain degree of manual dexterity, he can be given material of different textures to provide a variation of sensory experience. This type of stimulus material is another example of how very simple stimulation can bring profound effects in terms of early sensory experience, upon which the child can later build dynamic and rich sensory concepts.

Objects inside the Crib

In addition to suspended objects, objects can be left in the crib for the child to touch, explore, and manipulate. Small dolls, rubber cubes of bright colors, and squeeze toys can provide the child with an opportunity to explore interesting objects more closely. Objects should be relatively simple in shape, and they should be attractive to look at and to touch. An advantage of in-crib objects is that the infant can readily put them in her mouth. Researchers have found the sucking response to be one of the most significant perceptual developments of early infancy. Many observers see the mouth as being the center of perceptual activity in early infancy and an integrating element of the infant's perceptual and motor abilities.

Activities:
Five Months to
One Year

The highchair or infant's seat can be a very significant educational environment, for it is in a sitting position that the infant can be introduced to a great variety of stimulating learning activities. For the following activities, the child should be seated comfortably at a height which is appropriate for his gaining access to objects on a table. The sitting position provides the infant with a whole new view of the world: the world of horizontal expanse.

Colorful Cubes

Small, colorful cubes can be extremely valuable objects for training the infant's attention and for developing grasping ability. Rubber cubes have certain advantages, especially because of their appropriateness to being placed in the mouth. You might want to begin your activities with only one cube, presenting it on the table and moving it about. It is fascinating to watch the infant following the cube with his eyes and his upper body. Through continual repetition, the child will increase his attention span and concentration. You can gradually increase the speed of movement. Then additional cubes can be used, preferably of different colors, but cubes should be of the same size to facilitate the development of a first successful grasping response. Later different sizes can be added.

Slowly the child will begin to reach out for the cubes and attempt to grasp them; success usually comes between the third and fifth month. This development of reaching and grasping responses is extremely important in the environmental awareness of the child. It is through reaching and grasping for objects that the child masters the nature of near space, develops an interest in exploration, and expands his repertoire of, and ability for, basic perceptual-motor coordination.

Reaching for objects, such as cubes, begins very early, but grasping is much more difficult. It comes as the culmination of a rather lengthy trial-and-error process. Motor coordination develops from the shoulder and arm, and then gradually to the hands and fingers. At first, you will probably have to attract the child's attention by moving the cube about or tapping it on the table. Eventually, the child will develop the ability to manipulate the cube himself, move it about, pick it up, and throw it down; such activities soon become self-reinforcing. This type of activity will become an important source of early childhood mastery, as the child becomes increasingly able to manipulate things in his environment, to reach and grasp at will, and to be the cause of environmental variation. From this point on, the direct intervention of the adult will become progressively less important as the child himself becomes increasingly able to create his own diversity and, by acting upon experience, can create new experience.

The Spoon and Rattle

A simple household object like a spoon provides the young child with an interesting variation on the cube. The spoon must be grasped in a completely different way than the cube. Initially, it might be helpful for you to hold the spoon and show the child how it can be very easily banged on the table with interesting results. It is interesting to watch the development of the full closure of the hand required to grasp the spoon. A rattle can also provide a novel stimulus for grasping. In addition, it can reinforce the actions of the child with sound.

It is most interesting to witness the development of the grasping response. First, the infant explores the object visually. Then she begins to reach for it. Slowly, by trial-and-error, the child develops an ability to move the object, then wrap her fingers around an appropriate part, and grasp it. Finally, she is able to lift the object and use it.

Obtaining an Object Attached to a String

Obtaining an object using another is an important step in developing problem-solving ability and insight. The child may have had numerous previous experiences in not being able to retrieve objects outside of his immediate reach. This activitity indicates to the child a method for obtaining such an object. For example, a rubber ring is placed outisde of the child's reach. A piece of string is attached to the object, after the child has had the chance to view the ring and attempt to reach for it. The string is placed in the hand of the child, and he is shown how tugging on the string will bring the ring closer to him, within his reach. Soon, the child will probably be able to pick up the string himself and independently draw the object within his reach, eventually grasping it.

Mirror Play

The mirror can provide the infant with her first opportunity to see herself. The child may respond to her image by smiling, reaching for, and perhaps patting the image. Through the continued use of the mirror, the child will begin to recognize the movements she makes in response to her own image. She may begin to better understand her new abilities to act upon her environment. Children have also been known to start talking to their reflections. This activity is a very healthy and enjoyable one for the infant and fascinating for the parent, as the child gradually develops increasing self-recognition.

Hide and Seek

Developing a concept of object permanence can be facilitated through a continual game of Hide and Seek. This will aid the child in the realization that objects may be covered, but they are still *there*. Placing objects behind larger objects, placing a cloth over objects, and other related activities can help the child develop this important notion of an enduring world which does not disappear when it can no longer be seen.

At first, you can partially hide an object, preferably one that is very attractive. The child will eventually retrieve it. Then, gradually, the entire object can be hidden from sight. This activity can be structured in such a way that the child can be led from very simple to more difficult tasks. It will be a valuable exercise for stimulating the child to start "thinking" about the nature of his world, a world that is gradually developing new meaning and stability. Object permanence is a first step toward an enduring reality and a significant step toward intellectual growth.

Further Reaching and Grasping Activities

It is through reaching and grasping activities that the child develops her ability to manipulate her environment. The more experience the child has with a large variety of different objects, the more sophisticated her reaching and grasping ability will become. This will soon be translated into richer exploratory endeavors as the child learns that manipulating objects is an efficient way to investigate the world.

Any number of objects are appropriate for early grasping experience. Highly recommended are cubes, small boxes, spoons, rings, clothespins, rattles, dinner bells, and other similar objects. Eventually, the child will progress to finer manipulation of smaller objects. Whenever possible, it is advantageous to integrate a number of related activities, such as grasping a squeaking toy or manipulating objects with different textures. It is through such integrated experience that the young child can develop a greater understanding of the diverse characteristics of things.

Placing a Cube into a Cup

Through the development of placement ability and releasing an object accurately, the child increases his manual dexterity, his perceptual abilities, and his hand-eye coordination. Placing wooden cubes into a metal cup is an ideal activity for fostering this learning. This is a rather simple activity once the child masters it, much like target practice at first. Soon the child becomes able to develop his manual skills to the point at which he can grasp and release objects with practically no effort at all. In the meantime, it is important for him to practice grasping activities with a variety of objects. This activity can be increased in difficulty by using a smaller cup or a larger cube, but care should be taken, as always, not to make the activity too difficult at first. The repetition of this activity can contribute significantly to the child's sense of physical mastery, self-effectiveness, and competence.

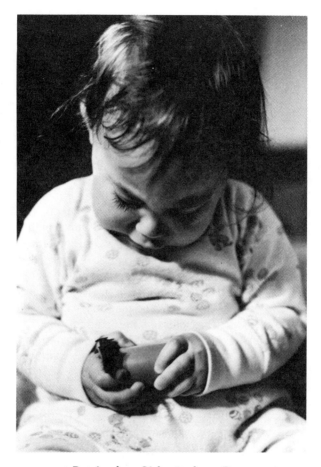

Replacing Objects in a Box

It is an interesting experiment to keep the objects used for the above activities together in a box and ask the child to help you replace them after activities are completed. Later, this same type of activity can be extended to the replacement of objects to specific places around the house.

Early Sensory Training Activities

Although most sensory learning and exploration will come during the second and third years, some important activities can be introduced during the second half of the first year. It is important to give the child an opportunity to experience different sensations as early as possible. There are splendid opportunities for sensory experience in the integration of activities for developing grasping abilities. Examples of such activities are grasping objects with different tactile qualities, banging objects against other objects, shaking sound boxes and rattles, and playing with various types of dry food and play dough. The choice of materials is extremely important; they should be attractive, appropriately complex, stimulating to the touch, and colorful. Futhermore, the selection of stimulating materials from around the home is an enormously creative experience.

The infant will particularly enjoy the opportunity to play with materials of different textures, for touch is an extremely significant part of infancy. In a real way, every manipulative activity of infancy is a novel sensory experience with very important tactile components. But this early tactile experience can be greatly expanded by not limiting the child only to solid materials which can be grasped. It is also important to let the child experiment with materials that he cannot so readily pick up, materials that he can run through his hands, materials with different consistencies. The relatively free-form experience with materials such as rice, sugar, flour, sand, dry foods, liquids, and play dough can help to develop exploration and creative self-expression in the child. Exploring with the young child the many textures and consistencies of materials around the house is a revelation. Young children love to fill containers and dump them out again. Give the young child a scooper and some liquid or granular substance, and magic begins.

Another of the great pleasures of infancy is sound. The infant loves to listen to different sounds and make them himself. This interest can be used creatively by making sound boxes: filling small containers with different materials, taping them closed, and presenting them to the child. At first you can shake them for the child, but eventually he will do it for himself. Creating sounds is an important part of his developing sense of self. There is perhaps no other activity that gives the child such immediate feedback that he is a "cause" than the creation of sound by shaking a sound box, a bell, a rattle, squeezing a squeaking toy, or hitting an object against another.

Activities:
One Year to
Five Years

The following activities should be viewed primarily as "ideas," not as a comprehensive program of action. There are no two children who are identical, and this is the way it should be. In order to recognize this individual uniqueness, it is important that a program be specifically developed for each child. *This is your job.* Use these suggestions but try not to be satisfied with them and use them with care and skepticism. The great value of these suggested activities is that they can provide a "jumping off point" for so many other possibilities. This is a magnificent opportunity for the adult to become an educational designer.

There are just a few other suggestions which might be in order here:

1. Always begin each activity by showing the child how it is to be done.
2. If the activity proves to be difficult, there is no reason to stick to the recommended procedures. Simplify the activity if you can. If not,

try some other activity more appropriate to the child's interests and readiness level.

3. Each child reaches her level of readiness for certain activities at a different rate, and each child has certain abilities, and often certain disabilities. Be diagnostic in your supervision; help the child when she needs help, but let her be as independent as possible.

4. You can add a new dimension to the suggested activities by introducing a time factor when the child becomes proficient.

5. Concentrate on helping the child become really good at a few activities and try not to move her on to others before she is ready. The development of self-confidence and feelings of mastery should be considered the foremost objective of these activities. You can always gradually increase the difficulty levels of activities, as appropriate.

6. You can add another dimension to the suggested activities: gradually build the child's memory by asking questions about the activity after it has been completed. This also can be done by seeing if the child can remember the activity directions at a later time.

7. Use any opportunities you can find for extending the scope of these activities. For instance, use the kitchen to its educational potential. Make sure the child helps out, samples different foods, identifies familiar smells.

8. Finally, and most importantly, be creative. Hopefully, the suggested activities will stimulate your own imagination. If you use these opportunities, the preschool educational experience can be the richest of your life, and certainly in the lives of your children. Point out and explore the textures, shapes, colors, and functions around the house or room that are too often taken for granted but represent the most significant educational resources we have for early childhood enrichment.

Suggested Materials

Water	Index Cards
Sand	Elastic
Cardboard	Golf Tees
Cubes and Blocks	Dry Foods
Cardboard Boxes	Small Cereal Boxes
Magnifying Glass	Pie Pans

Paste
Scraps
Sandpaper
Household Containers
Tape
Clay
Play Dough
Paints
Crayons
Prisms
Scissors
Coins
Jars and Lids
Paper Towel Rolls
Toilet Paper Rolls
Blindfold
Cellophane
Egg Cartons
String and Rope
Beads
Balls
Felt
Leather
Tree Branches
Tree Bark
Construction Paper
Paper Plates
Paper Cups
Spoons
Toys
Keys

Match Boxes
Film Boxes and Cans
Mirror
Popsicle Sticks
Tongue Depressors
Straws
Sugar Cubes
Toothpicks
Clothespins
Pipe Cleaners
Spools
Fabric Samples and Scraps
Rocks and Stones
Paint Samples
Yarn
Wall Paper Samples and Scraps
Wrapping Paper
Ribbon
Lace
Shoe Laces
Cotton Balls
Gauze Pads
Leaves
Picture Books
Flowers
Panty Hose Eggs
Washers
Buttons
Brown Wrapping Paper
Models
Magazines

Which Objects Are the Same?

Find numerous small objects. Objects with very obvious distinctive features will work best, especially in the early stages of this activity. *Suggested objects include:*

Clothespins
Spoons
Yarn

Paper Clips
Checkers
Poker Chips

Pens	Small Containers
Thimbles	Funnels
Empty Thread Spools	Scoopers
Napkins	Buttons
Corks	Vegetables
Bottle Caps	Rubber Balls

These are just some suggestions, but the list of possible objects to use in this activity is as large as your imagination.

Directions

Lay the objects selected out on a table within easy reach of the child. Arrange objects in random order. Begin the child with only four objects (two sets of the same object) and have her place the same objects together in a group. Later, it will be easy to expand the activity to three pairs of objects and more. You can also advance to groups of three or more of the same object and even begin to add "distractors," objects which cannot be paired with others.

This activity will help the child learn to group objects which look alike and is basic for practicing association and discrimination. It will give the child an opportunity to use her perceptual abilities in perceiving similarities and differences of objects in her environment. Soon this type of activity can be expanded to almost all objects.

Which Colors Are the Same?

There are a number of methods of presenting this activity. You can make Color Cards, use colored yarn, colored chips, paint, wallpaper samples, or just pieces of colored construction paper. Any brightly colored materials can be used. Materials should be large enough at first so that the child will have no difficulty seeing and manipulating them. Color Cards are particularly useful because they can be used over and over again, and there are no extraneous attributes which might distract the child's attention.

Making Permanent Color Cards

1. Obtain clear plastic, self-adhesive shelf liner.
2. Obtain any type of paper which comes in a great variety of rich and brilliant colors.
3. Cut the colored paper to playing-card size.
4. Cut the shelf liner to approximately the same size; try to keep it slightly bigger than the paper, rather than smaller.

5. Cover both sides of the colored paper with the clear plastic shelf liner. You can smooth out any air bubbles by rolling it with a rolling pin.

6. Trim off any excess plastic, and you will have Color Cards for your permanent use. They will be almost impossible to destroy!

Directions

The idea behind this activity is to have the child match the colors which are the same: red with red, green with green, blue with blue, etc. As a result, you should make duplicate Color Cards. The best way to begin this activity is to lay out three or four Color Cards; then give the child the duplicate cards for those colors and have him match them. You can gradually increase the difficulty of the activity by increasing the number of colors to be matched and by adding distractors. You can gradually introduce more subtle color differences as the child becomes more experienced in his perceptual discrimination abilities.

This activity will help the child to practice his associative and discriminative abilities in color perception. Children enjoy this activity at all ages. However, be sure that you are not presenting too many choices too soon or forcing the child to make subtle color discriminations before he is ready to do so. You will eventually discover colors even *you* did not know existed.

Which Shapes Are the Same?

Follow the directions for making Color Cards and make a set of Permanent Shapes. All you need to do is cut out some basic shapes (square, rectangle, circle, triangle) using construction paper, cover them with plastic shelf liner, and then trim the excess plastic. The result will be a series of shapes, which the child can touch as well as see. Make a number of shapes of each type and use several colors for each shape. You can also make shapes of different sizes to further enhance the activity. However, at the beginning, this activity should be restricted to shape matching only, then gradually you can introduce other attributes such as color and size.

Directions

Lay out the four shapes (square, rectangle, circle, and triangle) on the table. Show the child how she can feel, as well as see, the differences in shape. Show her how you can count the number of sides. Lay shapes on top of each other to illustrate relationships. Show the child all the ways she can compare the figures. Then ask her to match the shapes one at a time. If she is wrong just show her the distinctive features of each shape again. Repeat the process for each of the shapes. Then you can let the child match all the figures when they are presented to her in one heap, pairing each shape. After a while, you can add distractors which cannot be paired or present groups in which there may be three or more members. You may also want to increase the number of shapes included by adding rhombuses, crosses, half circles, ovals, stars, different types of triangles, and others.

This activity will help the child to investigate the nature of shapes. Shapes are vitally important for our recognition of the things around us. Eventually, you can explore with the child, finding objects which approximate the geometrical shapes with which she has become familiar.

Which Textures Are the Same?

Children are very sensitive to tactile stimulation; they enjoy touching things and comparing sensations. You can create Texture Cards by cementing various materials with different textures to pieces of cardboard. Of course, you can use the many different textures of sandpaper available (there must be more than twenty different types); yet there are a multitude of other textures you can select. Examples are pieces of fabric, cotton balls, toilet tissue, paper towels, leaves, flowers; but possibilities are virtually unlimited.

Directions

Blindfold the child and ask him to touch the various Texture Cards. Then direct him to sort the cards into groups of the same textures. In order to do this, you will need duplicate textures. You can begin with just a couple of samples and then move on to activities in which there are many different textures from which to choose.

The sense of touch is a very important one for the young child, and many of his most meaningful investigations are tactile. A wonderful feeling of accomplishment results from the ability to isolate one sense and explore its potentialities. This is very much the case in this activity. As the child completes each instance of this activity, you can remove his blindfold so that he can see his achievement.

Which Designs Are the Same?

Cut simple designs out of magazines or draw them yourself. It is important that designs be simple and not have too many different elements at first. Wallpaper samples can be used very effectively. You might want to mount the designs on cardboard with rubber cement, especially if you plan to use them over and over again. You can gradually lead the child from simple to more complex instances by varying different design elements from time to time, including color or texture.

Directions

Lay out a set of designs and ask the child to match them with another set of the same designs. Start with only a few matches and then gradually introduce others. Show her what to look for. Ask her which designs she likes best.

   Through the use of this activity the child can explore a great number of visual stimuli, including form, color and texture, in addition to designs. This may also be a valuable exercise in aesthetic appreciation.

Which Pictures Are the Same?

Cut appropriate pictures out of magazines. Select pictures which feature distinctive people, animals, or objects that will interest the child. You can mount these pictures onto cardboard with rubber cement in order to prevent their destruction with frequent use. Find other examples of the same subjects so that the child will be able to match them. Be sure the similarity is obvious. One way to assure that the child will have little difficulty is to select pictures from the same advertising that is repeated in many publications. Or else, you can buy duplicate copies of a few magazines. Gradually, you can make the activity more difficult by selecting pictures that are slightly different. This is an excellent way to gradually direct the child to a realization of the existence of classes of similar things.

Directions

Lay out a set of pictures and have the child match a duplicate set with those already laid out. Show the child how it is done at first and point out important elements and characteristics of each. If there are objects around similar to the ones in the picture, show them to the child. This will illustrate the relationship between pictures and real objects. If the child is wrong, find out why, and show him the correct response. This activity can be made very challenging by adding distractors and by using objects which are similar but very different in some respects. You can also vary the background upon which the pictures are mounted or increase the number of matches to each group.

This activity is potentially quite a difficult one because there are so many possible distracting elements. The child is no longer matching only one isolated sensation but a complex combination of sensations that form pictures. The key to leading the child to success in this activity is to find pictures that are very bright and colorful and that emphasize the distinctive features of the subject. Cartoons are most appropriate.

Which Sounds Are the Same?

This activity is aimed at helping the child learn to listen more carefully and to discriminate better among sounds. Children enjoy the opportunity to listen to different sounds. Soon you will find the child "listening" to everyone and everything very carefully. It is quite amazing how such activities stimulate the child's interest. It is almost as if you released a great new power that had been long inhibited.

Making Sound Boxes

1. Take a milk carton or a Quaker Oats carton (really any container will do) and cover it with brown wrapping paper.
2. Place distinctive sounding substances into each carton.
3. Seal the carton with masking tape.
4. Make many sound boxes of many different sounds if you like, but remember that they can always be reused.

Directions

Show the child how she can shake the Sound Boxes to make distinctive sounds. Show her how the harder she shakes the box, the louder the sound is emitted. For this activity, you should make a number of duplicate Sound Boxes, the idea being to match similar sounds. Ask the child to indicate the sounds that are the same. You can start the child with just one or two simple choices and gradually progress to more and more difficult selections.

The sense of sound is an important one for the young child. Unfortunately, hearing is so rarely allowed to develop as an independent sensory modality. This is unfortunate for child and adult alike because so much pleasure can result from intelligent and varied auditory experience.

Which Tastes Are the Same?

Select foodstuffs which provide the child with broad experience with many different taste sensations. Choose salty, sweet, acid, sour foods.

Begin with tastes that are totally different and gradually introduce tastes which might be only subtly different. This will develop a discriminative ability in the child. It is quite extraordinary how uneducated most people are in terms of their sense of taste.

Directions

Blindfold the child or ask him to cover his eyes. Present different food-stuffs to him and ask him to indicate which tastes are the same. Start with only a few choices and then gradually build up the number of taste selections offered. You might also want to deal with substances which are very much alike in taste but which might have different appearances and textures, like different types of sugar.

The sense of taste is a very important one for the young child who loves to put things in his mouth. Taste is a very neglected human ability but a very important one. It will help the child gain a greater and more sensitive exploratory ability and will stimulate his curiosity about the variations in the world around him.

Which Smells Are the Same?

Children get a particular joy out of their sense of smell and very much enjoy the exploration of the smells around them. The variety of smells in the environment is really remarkable. Think of all the variety of smells in flowers alone.

Directions

Blindfold the child and ask her to match the different smells you will be presenting to her. You will find that the child will rapidly become quite adept at this activity; maybe even better at it than you! There is a tremendous built-in motivation potential for this activity due to its natur-ally pleasing tasks.

Which Objects Are the Same Size?

Size is quite a difficult concept for the young child to master but is an extremely important one. However, comparisons on the basis of a charac-teristic such as size are more difficult for the young child than those based on form or color. Be certain, at least at the beginning stages of this activity, that objects vary in size on only one dimension; otherwise, the child will not know where to look for size clues.

Directions

Select containers around the house that vary in size on one dimension, like length only or width only. Select objects like different length straws and toothpicks. Ask the child to choose items which are the same size. Select comparisons that are very obvious at first.

Size comparisons are extremely important in training the child's visual-perceptual abilities. It is also important as a step toward developing thinking processes. Size is more abstract a comparison than shape or color, and care must be taken in this activity, but the readiness of the child for it will soon become evident. This activity will assist the child in developing finer and finer perceptual discrimination abilities.

Heaping into Groups

This activity represents one of the first substantive steps on the road to successful conceptualization. It is in this activity that the child can experiment with all different combinations of object groupings in a relatively free-form way. As a forerunner to more sophisticated concept formation, this activity is extremely significant, and considerable time should be spent on it. It is in this activity that the child can try out all her own ideas on grouping, subjective and objective.

Directions

Lay out a great variety of distinctive objects on a table; make sure that there are duplicates, even triplicates, of some of them. Be certain there are many different ways that the objects can be grouped, by type, color, shape, texture, etc. Use any objects that you feel might be appropriate. Talk to the child about the objects, look at them with her, touch them, explore them. Have the child group them in any groups she sees fit, using any criteria.

The implications of this activity are enormous, for it represents the most fundamental aspect of concept formation: the exploration of experimentation with, and subsequent development of, classifications. It is through this activity that the child can first explore the great variety of object groupings that can exist. This activity should be repeated over and over again with the same and different objects. Try not to move on to new objects until the child has had the opportunity to explore the limits of those initially presented. Repetition is a very significant part of this activity, especially for the child's feelings of satisfaction and mastery.

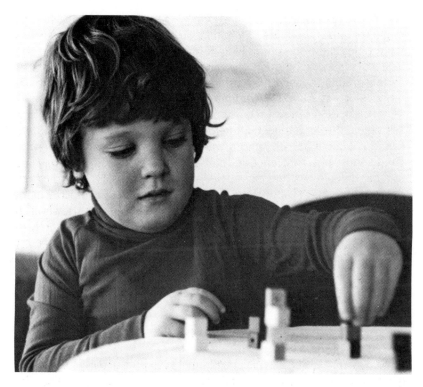

Water Play

Water play is an activity that children seem to enjoy a great deal, but few realize just how valuable a learning activity it is. Through the process of experimenting with water, the child learns about the nature of liquids and how they can be made to fit any shape, depending on the container they are put into. It integrates the intellectual curiosity of the child with practice in motor coordination. Find a variety of diverse containers; glass containers are best. Select containers of different shapes. The child can fill containers by "scooping" water into them with an eyedropper, by immersing them in water, or by pouring water into them, directly and with a funnel. Water play is relatively free form, creative, manipulative, and lots of fun.

Directions

Fill a rather large basin with water. Present the child with the water and a number of different types of containers, measuring cups, measuring spoons, regular spoons, cans, strainers, and other materials that you might feel are appropriate. It might be wise to begin this activity with very few articles and gradually build up to many different containers and other devices for experimentation. It is most beneficial to talk to the child about certain effects and relationships and call his attention to specific characteristics of water and the containers.

This activity is a very important and multi-faceted one. It encompasses a great deal of intellectual, perceptual, and motor learning. Children love this type of activity, and it will contribute significantly toward the child's sense of competence and self-effectiveness. There are a very large number of learnings that can center around this activity, including concepts of *fullness, shape, emptiness,* and *weight* and comparisons between containers with different amounts of water in them. However, be sure that when you are comparing containers they are approximately the same size, because the young child is probably not yet able to cope with the comparison of liquid in containers of different sizes and shapes. This is the previously mentioned Piagetian problem of learning conservation of quantity.

Sand Play

Sand play, like water play, is an extremely valuable activity that encompasses a great deal of intellectual, perceptual, and motor learning. Children love to play with sand, but on the beach their experimentation is usually quite limited. At home or at school, the child can experiment with filling all different types of containers and scooping with different utensils. There are a large number of activities that can center around exploring the nature of sand, comparing its characteristics with other materials, and investigating its properties. Sand can be bought in many different textures. It presents enormous possibilities for the creative development of learning activities that are highly manipulative, constructive, and stimulating.

Directions

Fill a large box or basin with sand (most building supply dealers stock it). Present the child with a number of containers and utensils she can use for filling them. Small boxes, buckets, bottles, cans, scoopers, spoons, measuring cups and spoons are most appropriate for this activity. Use your imagination to devise creative ways for the child to experiment with sand. Help her understand the potentials and limitations of the material. Point out important lessons as they arise during the course of the activity.

Musical Instruments

Children love music, and they love to make music. These natural, expressive desires can be used to encourage the child's creativity, to discuss the nature of sound, and to classify types of sounds and music. No specific method and no specific directions are suggested for this type of activity. Use your own imagination to design activities around the use of simple musical instruments, or just let the child play with them and learn from simple exposure to a wide variety of musical sounds. Simple instruments that are suggested for these activities are:

Different types of drums (or even boxes that can be hit)
Tambourine
Triangle
Blocks (just banging them together)
Sand Blocks (just wooden blocks with sandpaper attached)
Finger Cymbals
Spoons
Wind Chimes
Whistle
Beads and Buttons in a Jar
Squeaker Toy
Water-filled Glasses tapped with a spoon (different
   amounts of water make the glasses sound differently
   when tapped)

Also, you can explore with the child to discover your own, original musical instruments.

Measuring

Measuring is a very practical and useful activity for the child and can be used as the basis of any number of other investigations. The idea behind this activity is very simply to help the child understand the nature of size through measurement. This can be done by using all types of measurement devices to compare sizes. For instance, you can take a piece of string and use it to compare two or more objects to see which is larger and which is smaller. You can of course also use a ruler but do not really expect the child to understand the units of measurement. The focus of this activity should simply be on comparing sizes only.

This measurement activity can be used to classify items according to size or to order them according to size. Measurement can also be used in activities concerning the exploration of space and spatial relationships. Distances between objects can be measured, for instance, a table may be "two string lengths" from a door.

Something's Missing

This activity contributes significantly to the problem-solving ability and visual skills of the child. The idea behind it is to present the child with a picture from which an important element is missing. The child is expected to discover what part is missing and then replace it.

Directions

Construct a series of pictures of people, animals, or objects by cutting them out of magazines or picture books. You can mount each picture on cardboard, with rubber cement, before you cut it up. Once you have done this, you should cut a part off the subject. Ask the child to replace the part selected from a group of possibilities, and perhaps talk to him about it. It may be necessary for you to demonstrate at first. Another possible use of this activity is for classification. For instance, you can ask the child to put all the similar missing parts together: all the arms, all the legs, all the heads, etc. In this way, the child will gain insight about conceptual groupings. He will be able to understand that different-looking things may be "functionally equivalent" for classification purposes.

Seasons and Holidays

This is not a specific activity but an opportunity to facilitate the child's exploration of the changing seasons and the holidays which form such an important part of any child's life. Such activities are particularly meaningful and relevant to the child; they represent an advantageous mixture of concrete and abstract learning, and they can encompass so many different areas of thinking and doing.

The specific activities relating to the seasons and holidays are completely up to you, however, here are a number of suggestions to start your creative thinking. Focus the child's attention upon specific aspects of seasons and holidays, especially those aspects that are most relevant to her lifestyle. You can collect pictures with the child, make artistic projects, write stories about things that happen in certain seasons or at holidays, explore the reasons why seasons occur, and investigate the history of holidays. This will motivate the child to question the things around her, help her understand cause-and-effect relationships, and help her gain more appreciation for some of the factors that affect her life. These types of activities are of particular value because they are so personal to the child. You can use variations on other activities and relate them to aspects of seasons and holidays.

Elastic Board

The Elastic Board can provide the child with experience in motor coordination, attention, and visual abilities and with an opportunity to produce creative designs. The Elastic Board is simply composed of colored pieces of elastic wrapped around nails or screws secured in a piece of plywood. Such a board can be constructed by tacking the nails or screws to the board at approximately equal intervals. The size of the intervals will probably depend upon the child's motor abilities at the time of use, but 1" or ¾" could probably be recommended for beginning the activities.

The essential idea for activities using the Elastic Board is to make interesting designs, simple at first, and perhaps complex later. The elastic is wrapped around the nails or screws to form any designs you wish. You can use elastic string, elastic bands, or any other elastic products. This activity is highly creative, as possible design combinations are enormous. The child can considerably increase his manual dexterity and eye-hand coordination through the use of the Elastic Board. It is a relatively free-form instrument that can be inexpensively made and be of enduring value for the child as an educational toy.

Peg Board

A very simple, inexpensive, and useful Peg Board can be made with squares of acoustic ceiling tiles, appropriately perforated, and golf tees of various colors. This will provide the child with an extremely versatile learning instrument. In addition to its obvious value for providing experience in placing the pegs in the holes, there are numerous other uses for the Peg Board. The child can make colorful designs; she can group the different colored pegs in specific areas on the tile; and she can copy designs. If you purchase a number of the tiles, you can devise a design on one and let the child copy it on another. This will aid the child in training her visual abilities, concentration, attention, and fine-motor skills.

Hook Board

The Hook Board is an extremely valuable instrument for grouping activities of all kinds and for aiding the child in developing his fine-motor coordination. The Hook Board is simply a piece of plywood, with screw-in hooks placed at intervals. The basic idea of the Hook Board is to permit the child to hang things on the same and different hooks, in order to explore, classify, and represent relationships. Almost anything can be hung, as long as it has a loop which can be placed on the hook. The intervals at which the hooks are placed, the number of lines of hooks, and the number of hooks per line will depend upon the type of materials you wish to use. There is no problem in changing the configuration of hooks as your needs change. A reamer, nail, or hand drill will begin a hole anywhere on the board into which a hook can be easily screwed.

Activities which might be most adaptable for use with the Hook Board are grouping and sorting colors or textures. Any grouping or sequencing activity would really be ideal. All you have to do is tape or glue a loop of wire to the back of the cardboard and "hook it." You can use the Hook Board for making up picture stories as well. This format permits great flexibility. It also allows the child to make his own creations with ease: grouping and regrouping, changing sequences, and recombining elements to his own desires.

Touch Boxes

Touch Boxes provide the opportunity for a wide variety of tactile experiences. The idea behind the use of Touch Boxes is to provide the child with an opportunity to explore objects and substances with her sense of touch alone. This will allow the child to develop a keener sense of touch with which to explore and investigate her environment.

Touch Boxes can be any type of box with a hole in the side, allowing the child to insert a hand in order to feel the contents. In constructing a Touch Box, you should firmly secure the top with masking tape. You might want to wrap the box with colored paper to make it more attractive to the child. You can place almost anything inside of the box and ask the child to determine what it is by just touching it. When the child gives the correct response, you can show her the item to reinforce her correct answer. Children enjoy using their sense of touch very much, and the use of the Touch Boxes usually becomes a favorite activity.

Creating New Colors

Children love to be creative. This activity provides them with an ideal opportunity to explore and create new dimensions of color. It is a very simple one: mixing finger paints, water colors, or vegetable coloring to invent new colors. This activity can also revolve around the use of colored cellophane and a flashlight (the more powerful the better). Different colors of light can be made by combining various colors of cellophane and shining the light through them. This is an excellent way to help the child understand the nature of color. Be sure to talk to the child about the various effects; relate new colors formed to existing colors; and consider such things as color brightness and light intensity.

Detective

In this activity, the child tries to find a hidden object. There are a number of variations on this activity which may be used, including giving clues, providing a map, giving instructions. This activity can make the child more aware of the types of things that exist in her environment and where they can be found. It also can provide her with a mental framework for solving problems in a systematic manner.

Directions

Ask the child to find a certain object or substance hidden somewhere. You can give her one hint to start and perhaps more hints or clues later. Be sure that you stimulate the child's curiosity. You can also provide the child with a simple map, discuss it with her, and then have her use it to locate the object. This activity can provide a valuable way to utilize new learning in a practical context, such as direction (left and right, forward and backward) or relationship (on top of, over, or under) or other instructions.

More than anything, this activity is a good context for using the child's natural problem-solving ability. She will experience a tremendous sense of satisfaction on finding the hidden object. It is also good to have the child locate objects in their "proper place," as well as those hidden elsewhere. The gradual elimination of hints is also valuable. Gradually, the child will need fewer clues in finding the hidden object.

Grouping Objects According to Similarities

In this activity, the child is introduced to the broader notion of "class equivalence." This activity is not concerned with things that are the *same*, but with things that are *similar*. This is a much more sophisticated type of classification. The idea in this activity is to put buttons with buttons, beads with beads, and checkers with checkers (or whatever objects you decide to use in this activity). The principal achievement is to be able to detect classes of objects, regardless of such distracting attributes such as size and color.

Directions

Ask the child to group similar objects. Show him what specifically you want him to do; point out the specific object characteristics; and illustrate their functions. You can also organize the activity to include as many "irrelevant" characteristics as you feel are appropriate for the child's level of conceptual development. For example, you can begin with objects that are the same color and size, then go on to objects that differ in size as well as type; then move on to objects that differ in size, color, and type. The idea is to gradually overcome purely obvious groupings on the way to more mature concept formation.

The principal educational idea behind this activity is to help the child gradually develop more mature concepts by ignoring the irrelevant characteristics and grouping objects according to the more abstract notion of object type. There are tremendous opportunities in this activity for the careful organization of materials in such a way that the child is led reliably to successful concept mastery.

Photography

Do you have an instamatic camera? Why not let the child take some pictures? Photography is a fascinating activity, fun and rewarding. Show the child how very easy it is to aim the camera and push the button. Have her practice at first without film; teach her how to hold the camera steady and how to isolate aspects of the environment to focus upon. Eventually, you can explore with the child and camera. Talk about what certain things would look like on film. Shoot a roll of film; get it printed; and discuss the experience. Shoot pictures which might form the basis of a photo essay. Take pictures of similar things which are part of the same conceptual grouping. Photograph moments of joy and exhilaration. The camera is one of the most effective tools for increasing the child's self-concept. What better way to reward someone than to capture a moment of success on film? Photography is a new and important method of expression; it is communicative and artistic. It is also within the capabilities of almost any youngster. Why not use it?

Magnifying

This activity centers around the magnifying glass, an extremely valuable educational tool which can be purchased in any variety store for less than a dollar. The child will gain a tremendous amount of pleasure investigating with the magnifying glass. Start him off by showing him how it is done, but, before long, he will be exploring, looking at everything in a completely different way. Plants and different types of foodstuffs make fascinating starting points for this type of activity. Perhaps the greatest benefit of this activity is an indirect one: the child will learn to concentrate on details and develop a greater attention span.

Copying and Tracing

This activity is an important one in the early years because it provides the child with an excellent opportunity to train her fine-motor coordination. There is nothing creative about copying or tracing shapes and figures, but it is an important step on the road to better perceptual-motor coordination, especially for eye, hand, and finger coordination.

Directions

This activity very simply includes presenting the child with simple geometrical shapes to copy and trace. Make certain that the figures are bold enough for easy tracing through lightweight tracing paper. At first, you might have to help the child, teach her to hold a crayon properly, and guide her hand. Gradually, she will gain more control. You can enhance this activity by integrating other elements into it, such as using many bright colors and talking to the child about them and by using different drawing instruments.

Grouping on the Basis of Function

The basic idea behind this activity is to help the child understand the nature of the uses of things. Show the child how to match by function.

Show him the functions of the objects being used in this activity. Select objects very carefully so that their function is obvious and familiar to the child. This activity need not take place in a confined area and can be the basis for an exploration of an area. "See this thing; see what it does. Let's see if we can find other objects that serve similar purposes." Containers, bottle openers, books, scissors, clothing, mirrors—the list of possible objects is unlimited. The only important thing is that the child be familiar with them. Objects to be considered should vary in some characteristic so that the child can see that they are part of the same functional class, although different in appearance.

Different Shades of the Same Colors

Color is an important part of aesthetic appreciation. It is also extremely adaptable to concept formation activities. This activity can be of great educational value to both adults and children. The basic notion of this activity is to present the child with practical experience in dealing with a great variety of instances of colors. Few people realize the incredible diversity of color, and rarely are children given the opportunity to explore color in any but the most cursory manner. For most, red is red and green is green, and this is unfortunate because it greatly limits our ability to perceive the diversity around us and appreciate it.

The possibilities for organizing this activity are virtually limitless. One suggested approach is to acquire paint samples (hundreds and hundreds of different shades are available) and yarn samples. There is an incredible amount of color diversity available from these two sources alone. The idea is to acquaint the child with the fact that red, green, and all other colors have a tremendous variety of shades and intensities. Present the child with a few different instances of the same color, maybe examples of red, blue, and green; then have the child group these instances of the same color together. Use your own imagination in developing this activity. You can eventually use as many colors and shades as you find appropriate. Talk with the child about the process of color categorization and about the diversity of colors and shades of colors available to her. Ask her what colors and shades she likes best. Another interesting variation on this activity is to have the child sequence different shades of the same color in order of their intensity and brightness. This is a good way to exercise the child's perceptual abilities.

Color is an extremely important visual sensation. However, many children are not given the opportunity to explore the tremendous variety of color experience. The appreciation of color is particularly valuable in developing aesthetic appreciation, and it is a very effective vehicle for the development of mature conceptual abilities. It is most appropriate to follow up this activity by discussing colors around the room or those in pictures, color relationships, and colors in terms of artistic appreciation.

Exploring Shapes

This activity is aimed at further developing the child's understanding of shapes, both in terms of geometric figures and as embodied in the world around him. Shapes are everywhere. Rudolf Arnheim even calls form the "perceptual carrier of meaning." In this activity, the child will explore shapes that are similar but may be different from each other in one way or another. This activity will present the opportunity for the child to explore unusual shapes, as well as the relationship of shapes to one another.

Directions

Cut out construction paper shapes of all types and sizes. You can make different types of triangles, rectangles, ovals, and other shapes. You can make them of different sizes, with different length sides. The basic idea is for the child to understand that triangles are three-sided figures, squares are four-sided figures with sides of equal length, rectangles have opposite sides of equal length, and other such learnings. Help the child categorize the similar shapes into groups, and discuss the distinctive characteristics of each. By working with the child, explaining certain things, and by giving the child experience with exploring, handling, and playing with different shapes, you will aid the child to gradually understand certain rules; and he will recognize certain regularities, similarities, and differences among shapes. The exposure to this type of diversity will create a valuable experiential background in this area.

Children love to deal with shapes. Shapes are simple to categorize, because their principal characteristics are so distinctive. It is the ease of shape categorizing and the rewarding nature of the activity that makes this type of learning so appealing to all concerned. There are tremendous opportunities to categorize and explore shapes in order to integrate more sophisticated learning and related topics as part of the activity. You can begin with simple shapes, move on to more complex shapes, add distracting elements like color and size, and help the child gain a real understanding of the nature of the problem. You can also combine shapes, make designs and mosaics out of shapes, and develop your own variations on existing shapes.

Matching Forms

This activity will help to develop the child's ability to understand the nature of shapes, increase visual acuity, and provide practice in hand-eye coordination. The activity is concerned with the child's placing cutout shapes in the proper place, within the figure's outline on a piece of poster board. The activity requires the child to place the shapes precisely within the outline of the shape and thus requires considerable visual ability and manual dexterity.

Directions

Cut various shapes out of poster board; be certain that they are large and colorful. Draw outlines of these shapes on a larger piece of poster board with bold lines. Show the child how to place the shapes within the borders of the outline in various ways. You can increase the difficulty of the shapes used as the child develops more competence in the activity. Obviously the difficulty of the activity is determined by the number of sides of the form, its irregularity, and its size. You can start out with simple shapes such as circles, squares, and triangles; then, you can gradually move on to such shapes as crosses, stars, parallelograms, and others. Use every opportunity to provide insights into the activity and the forms.

Chaining

The basic idea of this activity is to provide an exercise to allow the child to match objects on the basis of many different characteristics. This activity allows great flexibility, and it appears to represent an important step in the child's development to more sophisticated methods of conceptualization. In this activity, the child bases his matching on whatever characteristic he likes at a specific moment. He may begin matching on the basis of form, then decide to match on the basis of color, and continue to match on other different characteristics.

Directions

Ask the child to begin matching objects chosen from a heap of things. The heap can include any number of diverse objects, but the simpler the better, particularly at first. Start the child off by matching a form with a similar form or a color with the same color; then show the child how to continue to draw objects from the heap and place them on the end of the "chain," as long as it appears to be related in some significant way to the last item placed on the chain.

Through this activity the child moves from purely subjective matching to matching based on significant objective characteristics. This activity provides the flexibility that children appreciate. It also provides the child with an opportunity to explore a great variety of possible matchings. He can explore matching on the basis of shape, form, color, type, function, weight, size, and any number of other characteristics. It also provides him with an opportunity to exercise a degree of mental flexibility that is beginning to develop.

Parts of the Body

Learning the parts of the body is extremely important and useful for the young child. This activity represents just one way that this learning can be accomplished and is most valuable when used to introduce more realistic explorations and spin-off activities. It centers on the construction of simple "body puzzles" with which the child will be able to learn the relationships between body parts. This activity can be accomplished at almost any level of sophistication.

Directions

Construct a series of "body puzzles" out of colored cardboard or construction paper, featuring the most important human body parts. Make the body parts as distinctive as possible and large enough to be easily manipulated by the child. You can make any number of body parts at first but be sure to wait to use them until the child is ready and has had a chance to work with the more simple (and obvious) parts first. Use this activity to discuss with the child the functions of body parts; point to parts of her anatomy, and your own to illustrate your points. Show the child how to construct a person by placing the body parts in their proper places. Allow the child to repeat this activity, and many variations on it, as much as she likes.

This is a rather simple activity, but one with many different variations and extensions. Perhaps the most valuable aspect of the activity is the opportunity to discuss and to explore the real-life functions of the body. In addition, there is the possibility for this activity to be extended to one in which conceptual groupings of body parts are formed. You can have the child put different arms together, or legs, or heads, etc. You can show the child how different the same body parts can be on different individuals. You can also further expand this activity to include the correspondence between the same body parts on humans and animals.

Maze Game

This game is important for helping the child develop a concept of space and a knowledge of relationships within space. It is also valuable for helping the child exercise his motor coordination and visual abilities. The idea of this activity is for the child to find his way through a series of mazes and retrieve objects, located throughout the mazes, in the process.

Directions

Mazes can be constructed in a number of ways. Two methods are highly recommended: made with cardboard boxes or drawn on a large sheet of brown wrapping paper. Make the maze simple at first, and then gradually progress to more complex and difficult configurations. Perhaps the cardboard box maze would be the best one to begin with; the boxes should provide a continuous path, through which the child can proceed. The brown paper maze is most flexible and easy to construct, to store, and with which to create variations. Place objects or rewards at various places on the maze, and explain to the child that he is to collect them as he follows the path through the maze. Explain to the child that he is not to cross a solid line and only follow the designated path. Make the mazes as interesting and colorful as possible. Try interesting variations on this activity by making the maze into a town, with shops and a town hall and by giving the child a list of tasks to accomplish at various establishments as he passes through the maze. Another possibility is to have the child collect items that fit into certain conceptual categories as he passes through the maze.

Complementary Groups

This activity is concerned with the objects in the child's environment that go together in "sets." They do not necessarily look alike, feel the same, taste the same, sound the same, or smell the same, and, yet, they belong together for one reason or another. The relationship between complementary objects is usually *functional*. There are hundreds of such objects, and learning about these functional relationships is very rewarding for the young child. Some examples of complementary groups of objects you can use are: knives, forks, and spoons; pens and pencils; buttons and buttonholes; snaps and hooks; paper and paper clips; paper and envelopes; cups and saucers; hammer and nails; pieces of jewelry; ribbon and wrapping paper; and camera and film. These are but a few ideas of the types of things that can be used in this activity. They are things that are *used* together.

Directions

Perhaps the best way to introduce this activity is to illustrate various complementary relationships to the child. Show her how things that do not appear the same can be used together, and, as such, they become identified with one another. Then, you can present the child with an object and have her select its complements from a heap of many objects. You can also use pictures of objects.

Complementary groupings are abstract in the sense that they are not based on physical similarity. They are usually linked by function, rather than obvious similarities. Eventually, the child will be exploring to discover the complementary groupings of objects that you did not present. She might even be able to invent her own.

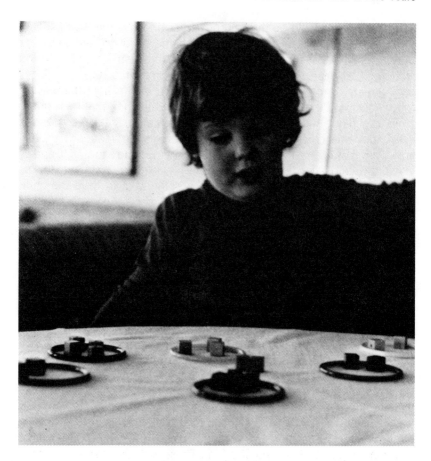

Collage Activities

The collage is a most creative and enjoyable learning activity. The combinations of diverse materials that form "works of art," a bulletin board, a
poster, or a fun design are tremendously motivating and rewarding. It is
somewhat sad that the value of this type of activity has been so infrequently recognized. The fun of collage making is second to none. It is an
activity that anyone can do well, regardless of artistic ability; and it is an
activity that is ideal for meaningful concept formation. Collages can be
made out of anything and everything: scraps of different types of paper,
tissue, cellophane, wrapping paper, fabrics, pieces of boxes, paper clips,
collections of pictures, clay, or any combination thereof. Just collect lots
of "things" and "stuff," and then paste them onto a piece of poster

board. You can be as simple or as creative as you want. The possibilities are enormous!

This activity should really remain as unstructured as possible in order to increase the potential for creativity on the part of the child. Perhaps the best way to start is to lay out many different types of scrap materials, of diverse shapes, colors, and textures, and then make a "scrap collage" by pasting them on a piece of poster board in random designs. At first, you can ask the child to help you; then, the child can take a more active role in the collage-making process, eventually taking over completely.

Collage making can be a learning activity through which the child explores the nature of diverse materials and investigates infinite combinations; it can represent the culmination of learning or the integration of previous exploratory activities into an enduring work of art. The emphasis in this type of activity should be on the use and consolidation of learning, as well as the encouragement of creative efforts. Hang the child's best efforts in his room and around the house. Show him how much you appreciate his work.

Sound Collage

If you have access to a tape recorder, this activity can be one of continuing enjoyment and learning. It is an activity that will allow adult and child to explore the auditory world in depth and gain a secure grasp on concepts of sound. This activity centers on the collection of sounds by use of the tape recorder, any and all sounds that we hear everyday. By recording them, we can isolate them, investigate them, and match them with their sources.

Directions

Explore all the sounds in your surrounding area. Go around with the tape recorder (have the child hold the microphone, if possible) and collect all the different sounds on tape. Some suggestions might be: electric appliances, pouring liquids, pouring cereals, flushing the toilet, typing, running water, or people's voices. These are just a few suggestions, but the list of possible sounds is virtually endless. Be creative, rub things against each other, shake things, make sounds any way you can. Have the child think up new ways to make sounds. Play back the sounds and see if the child can remember the source of each sound and perhaps discover what things make similar sounds.

Sounds are one of the "hidden educational resources." The simple technology of the tape recorder isolates these sounds and turns them into vital learning tools. There is no end to the combinations of sounds that can be created and stored for future reference. You can even make up stories using the tape recordings as sound effects.

Building Blocks

Children love building with blocks. Blocks can be used for developing fine-motor coordination, improving hand-eye coordination, providing classification activities, developing an elementary concept of number, or just for fun. Successful building with blocks gives the child an unequalled sense of self-effectiveness. Activities with blocks also have an advantage over many other tasks in that they can be either supervised or unsupervised, without fear of harm or frustration. Blocks are ideal materials of early childhood.

Show the child how blocks can be placed next to each other on a table and make attractive designs (especially if the blocks are multicolored). Show him how he can make a train by placing numerous blocks in a line, as long as he wants. Show the child how blocks can be stacked, one on top of another, until the "tower" falls. Show him how he can make pyramids, bridges, buildings, fences, and whole cities. Talk to him about the implications of the structures he makes. Ask him why a tower eventually falls. Why is it so hard to make a bridge with blocks? Show him pictures of real-life buildings, towers, and bridges in order to make the connection between the activity and the reality of the outside world. The number of possible structures that can be built with blocks is practically unlimited. There is also the possibility for exploring the different color formations that can be constructed with multi-colored building blocks. There is the opportunity to merge this activity with other classification activities. You can also discuss such concepts as *bigness* and *smallness*.

Enormous cognitive and psychomotor development can derive from activities involving blocks, in all areas of the child's development. Perhaps the greatest gains normally occur in the area of motor coordination. You can witness the gradual development of this coordination as the towers get bigger and the lines get straighter. No other activity fosters as much ego building as successfully constructing a house, bridge, or a tower, and then being able to build other taller or more elaborate ones.

Nest of Boxes

This activity is a very effective one for aiding in the development of fine-motor and hand-eye coordination in the child, as well as providing a foundation for object comparisons, particularly with respect to size and volume. The basic idea of this activity is simply for the child to fit successively smaller boxes inside of each other.

Directions

You can go to almost any department store and purchase a number of boxes which will fit inside of each other, if you don't already have them around the house. It is best when each successively smaller box is only slightly smaller than the next. You might want to begin this activity by showing the child precisely how the task is accomplished. It is probably best to begin with boxes that fit easily inside of each other, perhaps a box two or three steps smaller than the previous one. Present only a few boxes for nesting at first. Let her gradually build up her competence in this task. There is no rush for success; it is best to have the child repeat steps that she has mastered and consolidate this success. Talk to the child about the relationships among the boxes, in terms of size and volume. Show her how much each box can hold; compare them next to each other.

Obstacle Course

The child's motor coordination is closely related to his intellectual accomplishments. One of the principal feelings of early competence comes with the ability to move around easily and manipulate the environment. The Obstacle Course activity represents a significant step toward this mastery of motor coordination. The direct effect of this activity is a better understanding of how things in the environment are organized and what their relationships are to other things. This activity can also provide the basis for understanding such concepts as *over, under, through, inside, on top of,* just to name a few.

Directions

Cardboard boxes, especially big ones, are ideal for constructing an obstacle course environment for this activity. Place boxes all around a room, some stacked on top of each other, in such a way that the child must maneuver himself carefully in order to get to the other side of the room. All children seem to enjoy this very active type of activity that requires thinking as well as motor coordination. The more proficient the child becomes, the closer together you can place the boxes, until there is just barely enough room for the child to get between the boxes.

The Child's Corner

Children, like adults, need a place of their own, a place in which they are free to experiment and to be themselves. Such a personal area for the child can be a tremendous boost for her self-concept and self-esteem. Many people ignore this important facet of a child's life, the need for privacy and personal identification. Blow up a picture of the child to poster size (this can be done in most cities for a few dollars) and hang it in the "child's corner." The young child is highly dependent for most everything, and such a poster can be a tremendous boost for her ego. It will be a constant reminder that she is important.

The child's corner is a very important place. It is a place for independent discovery, for learning, and for growth. The corner should be stocked with meaningful items and materials with which the child can work on her own. Blocks, play dough, crayons and paper, objects of interesting colors, shapes and textures are perfect for the child to work with independently. As a result of this independent activity, she will become more self-reliant and confident in her abilities. Most of the activities suggested in this book center on the cooperative learning of parent and child together. However, there should also be the provision for independent activity, an important boost to the child's newly emerging self-concept.

Time Line of Achievements

An important contribution to the child's emerging self-concept is the recognition of the marvelous achievements that the child is accomplishing every day. The adult can greatly assist the child in developing a realistic sense of self-worth by keeping a record of major successes. An interesting way of doing this is through the use of a visual time line of these achievements. Pieces of colored construction paper depicting these accomplishments can be attached together and taped to the wall. For each major achievement, a new panel can be made. This way the child can see clearly the progress that he is making; it will be a great motivational device. It is like a growth chart for intellectual development. If the child has been successful at matching colors, a panel might pictorially depict this fact using the colors that the child has mastered.

Puzzles

Picture puzzles are simple to construct, fun to work with, and very significant practice for visual and motor skills. The puzzle is simply constructed by cutting up a picture from a magazine or picture book.

Try to find pictures that are large and simple, so that the child will have little trouble recognizing them. Pictures of familiar animals are usually excellent to begin with. Mount the pictures on cardboard to make them easier for the child to work with. Cut the puzzle into sections, at first two sections might be appropriate; then increase the number of puzzle parts gradually, as the child becomes ready for more. You can use the same puzzles over and over if you like, separating the picture into more and more pieces.

This activity can be a very challenging and rewarding one for the child. It can help to further refine her fine-motor coordination, as she places the puzzle pieces in their proper place, and increase her visual discrimination and recognition abilities. Gradually, as the activity progresses, the child will be more able to immediately recognize the picture, even before it has been put together.

Sequencing

This is a fairly advanced activity; it represents a sophisticated variation on the simpler grouping activities. In sequencing, the child sorts objects, substances, or other such things into a specific order, such as size, brightness or color, or number. Sequencing is a difficult activity largely because of the fact that the child must look at a number of aspects of the problem at once.

Sequencing, when used, should involve the gradual building of the child's ability. You can begin by asking the child which is bigger or which is brighter and gradually move from ordering two items to three, four, five, and even more. Sequencing activities can be integrated in many other activities discussed here, including those involving shape, size, consistency, sounds (loudness), space, and design (complexity).

The process of gaining fine perceptual-motor coordination is slow, but extremely important. Much growth in this area will occur naturally through the child's physical maturation, but it requires practice. Copying and tracing have proved excellent exercises for training fine hand-eye coordination. But remember the objective of this exercise, and try not to encourage tracing and copying after it has served its primary function. After that time, the *creative* and *independent* explorations of the child on paper should be encouraged as much as possible.

Caring for Plants and Animals

Living things provide the basis for great intellectual and emotional growth in the child. There is no other experience that seems to bring out more of the best in children than caring for living things, whether they be plants or animals. Such experiences give children a sense of importance, responsibility, and maturity, as well as a deep and enduring sense of personal satisfaction.

Even an experience as simple as caring for a small plant can be made into an extremely meaningful experience, if it is used properly. Such opportunities should be used to explain to the child about the nature of life, about how the plant grows, nurtured by light and water, and how, if it is not taken care of, it will die. You can also use the opportunity to explore different types of plants and animals, categorizing them and investigating their optimal conditions for growth.

Motor Activities and Body Movement

The following is a list of some of the motor activities that children seem to enjoy and benefit from most:

Touching
Rubbing textures
Grasping objects
Stringing beads
Sorting objects
Putting things back in their places
Building things
Catching balls
Throwing balls
Pulling toys
Reaching
Hitting things
Copying
Drawing
Placing objects
Sifting substances
Lifting things
Carrying things
Painting
Cutting with scissors
Lacing
Sweeping

Creeping
Tip-toeing
Walking
Running
Skipping
Hopping
Balancing on one foot
Jumping
Dancing
Kicking balls
Standing tall
Crawling
Kneading play dough
Watering plants
Helping in the kitchen
Hiding
Bending
Writing
Holding things
Imitating
Clapping
Tapping

Notes

Chapter 1

1. J. McV. Hunt, *Intelligence and Experience* (New York: The Ronald Press, 1961); D. P. Ausubel and E. V. Sullivan, *Theory and Problems of Child Development* (New York: Grune & Stratton, 1970).

2. L. D. Crow and A. Crow, *Child Development and Adjustment* (New York: The Macmillan Co., 1962), chap. 8.

3. R. H. Forgus, *Perception* (New York: McGraw-Hill, 1966).

4. B. S. Bloom, "Early Learning in the Home," paper presented at the University of California, Los Angeles (July 18, 1965; ERIC document ED-019-127).

5. A. Gesell, *Infancy and Human Growth* (New York: The Macmillan Co., 1928).

6. D. Russell, *Children's Thinking* (New York: Ginn and Co., 1956).

7. D. R. Spitzer, "What Is a Concept?" *Educational Technology*, July 1975, pp. 36-39.

8. Hunt, *Intelligence and Experience*, chap. 4.

9. Ibid.

10. A. Gesell, *Infancy and Human Growth*.

11. D. O. Hebb, *The Organization of Behavior* (New York: John Wiley & Sons, 1949).

12. R. W. White, "Motivation Reconsidered: The Concept of Competence," *Psychological Review* 66(1959): 297-333.

13. Ibid.

14. L. D. Crow and A. Crow, *Child Development and Adjustment.*

15. Ibid.

16. D. R. Spitzer, "What Is a Concept?"

17. Ibid.

18. D. Russell, *Children's Thinking,* p. 122.

19. R. W. White, "Motivation Reconsidered: The Concept of Competence."

20. Ibid.

21. R. H. Forgus, *Perception* (New York: McGraw-Hill, 1966), p. 274.

22. Ibid.

23. O. Lowenstein, *The Senses* (London: Penguin Books, 1966).

24. B. S. Bloom, "Early Learning in the Home."

25. Ibid.

26. M. D. Vernon, *The Psychology of Perception* (Baltimore: Penguin Books, 1962), chap. 2.

Chapter 2

1. M. Montessori, *The Discovery of the Child* (New York: Ballantine Books, 1967); M. Montessori, *The Absorbent Mind* (New York: Holt, Rinehart and Winston, 1967).

2. These names are mentioned to give the reader some familiarity with the people who have been the leaders in early childhood research. Hundreds of more names could easily be added.

3. These journals are listed to give the reader an idea of the number and variety of periodicals which have published a great majority of early childhood research over the years. This list is not intended to be exhaustive.

4. This list of organizations is provided to show the variety of organizations active today in the early childhood education area. This list is not intended to be comprehensive.

5. For an excellent discussion of Project Head Start, see M. Pines, *Revolution in Learning* (New York: Harper & Row, 1966), chap. 2.

6. Pines, *Revolution in Learning,* p. 24.

7. Ibid.

8. A. L. Butler, *Current Research in Early Childhood Education* (Washington, D.C.: American Association of Elementary-Kindergarten-Nursery Educators, 1970), pp. 42-43.

9. C. Bereiter and S. Englemann, *Teaching Disadvantaged Children in the Preschool* (Englewood Cliffs, N.J.: Prentice-Hall, 1966).

10. M. Almy, *The Early Childhood Educator at Work* (New York: McGraw-Hill, 1975), chap. 4.

11. J. McV. Hunt, *Intelligence and Experience* (New York: The Ronald Press, 1961), pp. 362-63.

12. W. Fowler, "The Effect of Early Stimulation in the Emergence of Cognitive Processes," in *Early Education,* eds. R. D. Hess and R. M. Bear (Chicago: Aldine, 1968), p. 17.

13. B. S. Bloom, *Stability and Change in Human Characteristics* (New York: John Wiley & Sons, 1964).

14. Ibid.

15. D. Elkind, *Children and Adolescents: Interpretive Essays on Jean Piaget* (New York: Oxford University Press, 1974).

16. E. L. Palmer, "Sesame Street: Shaping Broadcast Television to Needs of the Preschooler," *Educational Technology,* February 1971, pp. 18-22.

17. H. W. Stevenson, *Television and the Behavior of Preschool Children* (Minneapolis: University of Minnesota Press, 1971).

18. C. Gattegno, *Toward a Visual Culture* (New York: Outersbridge and Dienstfrey, 1969).

19. A new idea in visual education has emerged with the improbable label "visual literacy." See D. R. Spitzer and T. O. McNerny, "Operationally Defining Visual Literacy: A Research Challenge," *Audiovisual Instruction,* September 1975, pp. 30-31.

Chapter 3

1. J. McV. Hunt, *Intelligence and Experience* (New York: The Ronald Press, 1961), chap. 2.

2. Hunt, *Intelligence and Experience,* pp. 19-34.

3. Hunt, *Intelligence and Experience,* chap. 3.

4. W. Fowler, "The Effect of Early Stimulation in the Emergence of Cognitive Processes," in *Early Education,* eds. R. D. Hess and R. M. Bear (Chicago: Aldine, 1968), pp. 9-36.

5. J. Piaget, *The Construction of Reality in the Child* (New York: Basic Books, 1954). This theme also runs throughout Piaget's other studies.

6. J. Piaget, *The Psychology of Intelligence* (New York: Harcourt Brace Jovanovich, 1950).

7. Piaget, *The Construction of Reality. . . .*

8. Ibid.

9. Symbolic play is the child's first opportunity to "internalize" thinking and action. Piaget believes that such imitation is very crucial to development. See the excellent discussion of symbolic games in Hunt, *Intelligence and Experience,* pp. 180-85.

10. Memory provides the child with the beginnings of a realization that everything is not "here-and-now." See L. Braga and J. Braga, *Learning and Growing* (Englewood Cliffs, N.J.: Prentice-Hall, 1975), p. 97.

11. Piaget, *The Psychology of Intelligence.*

12. This is the predominant characteristic of the sensorimotor period, dependency on what the child sees directly. See M. D. Vernon, *The Psychology of Perception* (Baltimore: Penguin Books, 1962), p. 21.

13. The need for the child's own responsibility for his own learning is the most frequently recurring theme in Piaget's work.

14. See the excellent discussion of early memory in D. P. Ausubel and E. V. Sullivan, *Theory and Problems of Child Development* (New York: Grune & Stratton, 1957), pp. 601-6.

15. B. Inhelder and J. Piaget, *The Psychology of the Child* (New York: Basic Books, 1969), pp. 96-100.

Chapter 4

1. D. R. Spitzer, "What Is a Concept?" *Educational Technology,* July 1975, pp. 33-39. This article provides a comprehensive review of definitions of concepts.

2. J. S. Bruner, "On Going Beyond the Information Given," *Contemporary Approaches to Cognition* (Cambridge: Harvard University Press, 1957), pp. 41-69.

3. These are the author's own terms. They are used because they appear to make an important distinction between *mental concepts* and *environmental groupings,* both of which profoundly affect our thinking.

4. L. J. Stone, H. T. Smith, and L. B. Murphy, eds., *The Competent Infant* (New York: Basic Books, 1973). This is the most thorough compilation of, and commentary on, infant research that exists.

5. J. Piaget, *The Psychology of Intelligence* (New York: Harcourt Brace Jovanovich, 1950).

6. Ibid.

7. L. D. Crow and A. Crow, *Child Development and Adjustment* (New York: The Macmillan Co., 1962), pp. 188-89.

8. E. Sapir, *Language* (New York: Harcourt Brace Jovanovich, 1921). This is a fascinating account of the development of language and its importance.

9. D. P. Ausubel and E. V. Sullivan, *Theory and Problems of Child Development* (New York: Grune & Stratton, 1957), p. 555.

10. V. Lowenfeld, *Creative and Mental Growth* (New York: The Macmillan Co., 1957).

Chapter 5

1. A. Baldwin, *Behavior and Development in Childhood* (New York: The Dryden Press, 1955).

2. J. Piaget, *The Psychology of Intelligence* (New York: Harcourt Brace Jovanovich, 1950).

3. E. R. Hilgard and G. Bower, *Theories of Learning* (New York: Appleton-Century-Crofts, 1966).

4. This is referred to as *contiguity* in learning theory.

5. I. P. Pavlov, *Conditioned Reflexes* (London: Oxford University Press, 1927).

6. This is referred to as *extinction* in learning theory.

7. B. F. Skinner, *The Behavior of Organisms* (New York: Appleton-Century-Crofts, 1938).

8. P. H. Wolff, "The Natural History of Crying and Other Vocalizations in Early Infancy," in *Determinants of Infant Behavior IV,* ed. B. M. Foss (London: Methuen Publishing Co., 1969), pp. 81-109.

9. There is a general awareness that information derived from animal studies cannot be *directly* generalized to humans. However, such work is extremely valuable for accumulating evidence.

10. D. B. Ausubel and E. V. Sullivan, *Theory and Problems of Child Development* (New York: Grune & Stratton, 1957), pp. 703-4.

11. Ausubel and Sullivan, *Theory and . . . ,* p. 703.

12. B. F. Skinner, *The Technology of Teaching* (New York: Appleton-Century-Crofts, 1968).

13. This is the notion of *intrinsic motivation* discussed in Chapter 13.

14. B. F. Skinner, "Teaching Machines," *Science* 128 (1958): 969-77.

15. Ibid.

16. B. C. Mathis, J. W. Cotton, and L. Sechrest, *Psychological Foundations of Education* (New York: The Academic Press, 1970), chap. 11.

17. F. T. Tyler, "Issues Related to Readiness," in *Sixty-third Yearbook, National Society for the Study of Education,* ed. D. E. Griffiths (Chicago: University of Chicago Press, 1964), vol. 2, pp. 210-39.

18. J. McV. Hunt, *Intelligence and Experience* (New York: Ronald Press, 1961), p. 147. Hunt says, "environmental novelties are accommodated only as they are imposed."

19. Mathis et al., *Psychological Foundations of Education,* p. 449.

20. M. E. P. Seligman, *Helplessness* (San Francisco: W. H. Freeman & Co., 1974).

21. M. Montessori, *Dr. Montessori's Own Handbook* (New York: Schocken Books, 1965).

22. J. S. Bruner, "On Going Beyond the Information Given," *Contemporary Approaches to Cognition* (Cambridge: Harvard University Press, 1957), pp. 41-69.

23. D. O. Hebb, *The Organization of Behavior* (New York: John Wiley & Sons, 1949).

24. Ibid.

25. D. Russell, *Children's Thinking* (Boston: Ginn and Co., 1956).

26. L. D. Crow and A. Crow, *Child Development and Adjustment* (New York: The Macmillan Co., 1962), p. 188.

27. B. S. Bloom, *Stability and Change in Human Characteristics* (New York: John Wiley & Sons, 1964), p. 215.

Chapter 6

1. L. S. Vygotsky, *Thought and Language* (Cambridge, Mass: M. I. T. Press, 1962).

2. J. Piaget and B. Inhelder, *The Early Growth of Logic in the Child* (New York, W. W. Norton and Co., 1964).

3. However, Vygotsky presents a critique of Piaget's theory in his own book in Chapter 2.

4. J. Piaget, *The Psychology of Intelligence* (New York: Harcourt Brace Jovanovich, 1950).

5. This is a fundamental difference between *preconcepts* and *concepts* in both schemes; the difference is between planned grouping and fortuitous grouping (by chance).

6. J. McV. Hunt, *Intelligence and Experience* (New York: The Ronald Press, 1961), p. 258.

7. Vygotsky describes these early groupings as *syncretic conglomerations.*

8. Vygotsky, *Thought and Language.*

9. Vygotsky, *Thought and Language,* p. 61.

10. Ibid.

11. This is the idea, discussed earlier, that there are internal concepts (mental concepts) and external concepts (organization of the environment).

12. Vygotsky, *Thought and Language,* p. 65.

13. Piaget and Inhelder, *The Early Growth of Logic . . . ,* p. 45.

14. Piaget and Inhelder, *The Early Growth of Logic . . . ,* pp. 34-35.

15. Piaget and Inhelder, *The Early Growth of Logic . . . ,* pp. 53-54.

16. Piaget and Inhelder, *The Early Growth of Logic* . . . , pp. 34-35.

17. Abstraction is the key notion in concept formation theory. It is the ability to look at the properties of things apart from the objects themselves.

18. D. P. Ausubel and E. V. Sullivan, *Theory and Problems of Child Development* (New York: Grune & Stratton, 1957), p. 615.

Chapter 7

1. M. D. Vernon, *The Psychology of Perception* (Baltimore: Penguin Books, 1962), p. 17.

2. J. Piaget, *The Construction of Reality in the Child* (New York: Basic Books, 1954).

3. The reader can see this in any of Piaget's works, with his beautiful use of anecdotal records.

4. A. R. Jensen, "Learning in the Preschool Years," in *The Young Child,* eds. W. W. Hartup and N. L. Smothergill (Washington, D.C.: National Association for the Education of Young Children, 1967), p. 126.

5. Jensen, "Learning in the Preschool Years," p. 135.

6. D. P. Ausubel and E. V. Sullivan, *Theory and Problems of Child Development* (New York: Grune & Stratton, 1957), pp. 590-95.

7. Ausubel and Sullivan, *Theory and Problems* . . . , p. 556.

8. M. Almy, *The Early Childhood Educator at Work* (New York: McGraw-Hill, 1975), pp. 152-53.

9. Vernon, *The Psychology of Perception,* chap. 2.

10. D. O. Hebb, *The Organization of Behavior* (New York: John Wiley & Sons, 1949).

11. L. D. Crow and A. Crow, *Child Development and Adjustment* (New York: The Macmillan Co., 1962), p. 205.

12. B. S. Bloom, "Early Learning in the Home," paper presented at the University of California, Los Angeles, (July 18, 1965; ERIC document ED-019-127).

13. M. Montessori, *The Discovery of the Child* (New York: Ballantine Books, 1967).

14. W. Fowler, "The Effect of Early Stimulation in the Emergence of Cognitive Processes," in *Early Education,* eds. R. D. Hess and R. M. Bear (Chicago: Aldine Publishing Co., 1968), pp. 9-36.

15. Ausubel and Sullivan, *Theory and Problems* . . . , p. 572.

16. Ausubel and Sullivan, *Theory and Problems* . . . , pp. 539-41.

17. The author has observed this in West Africa (Senegal, Ivory Coast, and Ghana).

18. M. Young, *Buttons Are to Push* (New York: Pitman Publishing, 1970).

19. P. Torrance, "Factors Affecting Creative Thinking in Children," *Merrill-Palmer Quarterly* 7(1961): 171-80.

20. B. S. Bloom, *Stability and Change in Human Characteristics* (New York: John Wiley & Sons, 1964), p. 88.

Chapter 8

1. D. P. Ausubel and E. V. Sullivan, *Theory and Problems of Child Development* (New York: Grune & Stratton, 1957), p. 555.

2. M. von Senden, *Space and Sight* (New York: The Free Press, 1960).

3. B. S. Bloom, "Early Learning in the Home," paper presented at the University of California, Los Angeles (July 18, 1965; ERIC document ED-019-127).

4. M. D. Vernon, *The Psychology of Perception* (Baltimore: Penguin Books, 1962), chap. 2.

5. Ibid.

6. D. O. Hebb, *The Organization of Behavior* (New York: John Wiley & Sons, 1949).

7. Ibid.

8. D. E. Berlyne, *Conflict, Arousal, and Curiosity* (New York: McGraw-Hill, 1960).

9. R. L. Fantz, "Visual Perception from Birth as Shown by Pattern Selectivity," *Annals of the New York Academy of Sciences* 118 (1965): 793-814.

10. Ibid.

11. Ibid.

12. This appears to be the case for all learning: perceptual, conceptual, school learning, etc.

13. Ausubel and Sullivan, *Theory and Problems of . . . ,* pp. 556-57.

14. Ausubel and Sullivan, *Theory and Problems of . . . ,* p. 564.

15. Ausubel and Sullivan, *Theory and Problems of . . . ,* pp. 557-58.

16. Ausubel and Sullivan, *Theory and Problems of . . . ,* p. 557.

17. Vernon, *The Psychology of Perception,* pp. 21-22.

18. R. Forgus, *Perception* (New York: McGraw-Hill, 1966), chap. 6.

19. Ibid.

20. R. Arnheim, *Visual Thinking* (Berkeley: University of California Press, 1966).

21. B. C. Mathis, J. W. Cotton, and L. Sechrest, *Psychological Foundations of Education* (New York: The Academic Press, 1970), pp. 245-46.

22. Forgus, *Perception,* p. 1. Forgus defines *perception* as "the process of information extraction."

23. B. S. Bloom, "Learning in the Home," paper presented at the University of California, Los Angeles (July 18, 1965; ERIC document ED-019-127).

24. Ausubel and Sullivan, *Theory and Problems of . . . ,* pp. 703-4.

25. Ausubel and Sullivan, *Theory and Problems of . . . ,* p. 703.

26. Ausubel and Sullivan, *Theory and Problems of . . . ,* p. 601.

27. A. D. Woodruff, "Cognitive Models of Learning and Instruction," in *Instruction: Some Contemporary Viewpoints,* ed. L. Siegel (San Francisco: Chandler Publishing Co., 1967), pp. 55-98.

28. J. McV. Hunt, *Intelligence and Experience* (New York: The Ronald Press, 1961), pp. 126-29.

29. B. C. Mathis, J. W. Cotton, and L. Sechrest, *Psychological Foundations of Education* (New York: The Academic Press, 1970), pp. 164-68.

30. J. Piaget and B. Inhelder, *The Psychology of the Child* (New York: Basic Books, 1969), p. 83.

Chapter 9

1. O. Lowenstein, *The Senses* (London: Penguin Books, 1966), pp. 41-44.

2. Lowenstein, *The Senses,* chap. 3.

3. D. P. Ausubel and E. V. Sullivan, *Theory and Problems of Child Development* (New York: Grune & Stratton, 1957), p. 555.

4. R. Arnheim, *Visual Thinking* (Berkeley: University of California Press, 1969) and R. Arnheim, *Art and Visual Perception* (Berkeley: University of California Press, 1965).

5. Arnheim, *Art and Visual Perception,* p. 37.

6. Arnheim, *Visual Thinking,* chap. 7.

7. Ibid.

8. M. D. Vernon, *The Psychology of Perception* (Baltimore: Penguin Books, 1962), chap. 4 and R. Arnheim, *Visual Thinking,* p. 19, pp. 33-35, and pp. 66-69.

9. L. D. Crow and A. Crow, *Child Development and Adjustment* (New York: The Macmillan Co., 1962), pp. 182-89.

10. It is much more difficult for young children to develop *comparative* or *relational* concepts than *absolute* (concrete) concepts; these concepts usually do not start developing until the age of three.

11. See R. Arnheim, *Visual Thinking.*

12. B. S. Bloom, "Learning in the Home," paper presented at the University of California, Los Angeles (July 18, 1965; ERIC document ED 019-127).

Chapter 10

1. F. Caplan and T. Caplan, *The Power of Play* (New York: Anchor Books, 1974); R. E. Hartley, L. K. Frank, and R. M. Goldenson, *Understanding Children's Play* (New York: Columbia University Press, 1952).

2. A. Koestler, *The Act of Creation* (New York: The Macmillan Co., 1964).

3. D. E. Berlyne, *Conflict, Arousal and Curiosity* (New York: McGraw-Hill, 1960); D. O. Hebb, *The Organization of Behavior* (New York: John Wiley & Sons, 1949).

4. A. Koestler, *The Act of Creation.*

5. D. O. Hebb, "Drives and the C.N.S. (Conceptual Nervous System)," *Psychological Review* 62(1955): 243-54.

6. L. D. Crow and A. Crow, *Child Development and Adjustment* (New York: The Macmillan Co., 1962), pp. 211-13.

7. Crow and Crow, *Child Development . . . ,* p. 211.

8. E. P. Torrance, "Factors Affecting Creative Thinking in Children," *Merrill-Palmer Quarterly* 7(1961): 171-80.

9. J. S. Bruner, *Toward a Theory of Instruction* (Cambridge, Mass.: The Belknap Press, 1967), p. 96.

10. Ibid.

11. R. White, "Motivation Reconsidered: The Concept of Competence," *Psychological Review* 66(1959): 297-333.

12. M. Montessori, *The Absorbent Mind* (New York: Holt, Rinehart and Winston, 1967), chap. 2.

13. L. S. Vygotsky, "Play and Its Role in the Mental Development of the Child," *Soviet Psychology* 12(1966): 6-17.

14. D. P. Ausubel and E. V. Sullivan, *Theory and Problems of Child Development* (New York: Grune & Stratton, 1957), pp. 564-65.

15. C. C. Abt, *Serious Games* (New York: The Viking Press, 1970), chap. 1.

16. Caplan and Caplan, *The Power of Play.*

Chapter 11

1. P. Muller, *The Tasks of Childhood* (New York: McGraw-Hill, 1969).

2. W. R. Thompson, "Motivational Factors in Development," *Australian Journal of Psychology* 10(1958): 127-43.

3. M. Young, *Buttons are to Push* (New York: Pitman Publishing Corp., 1970), pp. 78-81. This entire book presents a fine treatment of parental encouragement of questions, discovery, and creativity.

4. M. Montessori, *Dr. Montessori's Own Handbook* (New York: Schocken Books, 1965).

5. J. S. Bruner, *Toward a Theory of Instruction* (Cambridge, Mass.: The Belknap Press, 1967), pp. 40-43.

6. The prerequisites of each exercise in Part Two are specified.

7. J. McV. Hunt, *Intelligence and Experience* (New York: The Ronald Press Co., 1961), p. 168. Hunt explains that adaptation requires a proper match between existing intellectual structures (schemata) and learning tasks.

8. E. P. Torrance, "Factors Affecting Creative Thinking in Children," *Merrill-Palmer Quarterly* 7(1961): 171-80.

9. The importance of examples, or *modeling,* is exemplified by the work of Albert Bandura. See, for example, A. Bandura, "Social Learning Through Imitation," in *Nebraska Symposium on Motivation, 1962* ed. M. R. Jones (Lincoln: University of Nebraska Press, 1962), pp. 211-69.

10. M. Montessori, *Dr. Montessori's Own Handbook.*

Chapter 12

1. M. A. Wallach, "Creativity and the Expression of Possibilities," in *Creativity and Learning,* ed. J. Kagan (Boston: Houghton Mifflin Co., 1967), p. 52.

2. J. P. Guilford, *On the Nature of Intelligence* (New York: McGraw-Hill, 1967).

3. Normative evaluation compares individuals with societal norms or standards.

4. F. Barron, "The Disposition Toward Originality," *Journal of Abnormal and Social Psychology* 51(1955): 478-85.

5. R. W. White, "Motivation Reconsidered: The Concept of Competence," *Psychological Review* 66(1959): 279-333.

6. J. Piaget, *The Psychology of Intelligence* (New York: Harcourt Brace Jovanovich, 1950).

7. D. C. McClelland, *The Achieving Society* (New York: The Free Press, 1967).

8. D. C. McClelland, "Toward a Theory of Motive Acquisition," *American Psychologist* 20(1965): 321-33.

9. F. Caplan and T. Caplan, *The Power of Play* (New York: Anchor Books, 1974).

10. B. Ghiselin, *The Creative Process* (Berkeley: University of California Press, 1952).

11. F. Barron, "The Disposition Toward Originality," 479-85.

12. R. Arnheim, *Visual Thinking* (Berkeley: University of California Press, 1969).

13. R. W. White, "Motivation Reconsidered: The Concept of Competence," *Psychological Review* 66(1959): 279-333.

14. V. Lowenfeld, *Creative and Mental Growth* (New York: The Macmillan Co., 1957), pp. 86-87.

15. Lowenfeld, *Creative and Mental Growth,* p. 86.

16. Lowenfeld, *Creative and Mental Growth,* chap. 3.

17. Lowenfeld, *Creative and Mental Growth,* p. 87.

18. Lowenfeld, *Creative and Mental Growth,* 15-17.

19. J. H. Di Leo, *Young Children and Their Drawings* (New York: Brunner/Mazel Publishers, 1970), p. 26.

20. Lowenfeld, *Creative and Mental Growth,* p. 93.

21. Lowenfeld, *Creative and Mental Growth,* p. 94.

22. Di Leo, *Young Children and Their Drawings,* pp. 28-35.

23. Di Leo, *Young Children and Their Drawings,* p. 35.

24. M. Young, *Buttons Are to Push* (New York: Pitman Publishing Corp., 1970).

25. J. Bruner, *Toward a Theory of Instruction* (Cambridge, Mass.: The Belknap Press, 1967), p. 96.

26. M. Wallach, "Creativity and the Expression of Possibilities," p. 52.

27. J. P. Guilford, *On the Nature of Intelligence.*

28. J. W. Getzels and P. W. Jackson, *Creativity and Intelligence* (New York: John Wiley & Sons, 1962).

29. M. A. Wallach and N. Kogan, *Modes of Thinking in Young Children* (New York: Holt, Rinehart and Winston, 1965).

Chapter 13

1. B. Weiner, *Theories of Motivation* (Chicago: Markham Publishing Co., 1972), chap. 1.

2. D. O. Hebb, *The Organization of Behavior* (New York: John Wiley & Sons, 1949).

3. D. E. Berlyne, *Conflict, Arousal and Curiosity* (New York: McGraw-Hill, 1960).

4. R. W. White, "Motivation Reconsidered: The Concept of Competence," *Psychological Review* 66(1959): 297-333.

5. J. McV. Hunt, "Motivation Inherent in Information Processing and Action," in *Motivation and Social Interaction,* ed. O. J. Harvey (New York: The Ronald Press, 1963).

6. C. Leuba, "Toward Some Integration of Learning Theories: The Concept of Optimal Stimulation," *Psychological Reports* 1(1955): 27-33.

7. A. H. Maslow, *Motivation and Personality* (New York: Harper & Row, Publishers, 1970).

8. E. L. Deci, "Effects of Externally Mediated Reward on Intrinsic Motivation," *Journal of Personality and Social Psychology* 18 (1971): 105-15.

9. Ibid.

10. H. A. Murray, *Explorations in Personality* (New York: Oxford University Press, 1938).

11. White, "Motivation Reconsidered. . . ."

12. W. F. Hill, "Activity as an Autonomous Drive," *Journal of Comparative Physiological Psychology* 49(1956): 15-19.

13. Hebb, *The Organization of Behavior.*

14. Berlyne, *Conflict, Arousal and Curiosity.*

15. Ibid.

16. Ibid.

17. J. W. Atkinson, "Motivational Determinants of Risk Taking Behavior," *Psychological Review* 64(1957): 359-72.

References

Intellectual Development

Beadle, M. *A Child's Mind.* New York: Jason Aronson, 1974.

Berlyne, D. E. *Conflict, Arousal and Curiosity.* New York: McGraw-Hill, 1960.

Bereiter, C., and Englemann, S. *Teaching Disadvantaged Children in the Pre-school.* Englewood Cliffs, N.J.: Prentice-Hall, 1966.

Bolton, N. *The Psychology of Thinking.* London: Methuen Publishing Co., 1972.

Bruner, J. S. "On Going Beyond the Information Given." *Contemporary Approaches to Cognition,* pp. 49-61. Cambridge, Mass.: Harvard University Press, 1957.

Bruner, J. S.; Goodnow, J. J.; and Austin, G. A. *A Study of Thinking.* New York: John Wiley & Sons, 1956.

Cattell, P. *The Measurement of Intelligence of Infants and Young Children.* New York: The Psychological Corporation, 1940.

Fowler, W. "The Effect of Early Stimulation in the Emergence of Cognitive Processes." In *Early Education,* edited by R. D. Hess and R. M. Bear, pp. 9-36. Chicago: Aldine Publishing Co., 1968.

Gesell, A. *The Mental Growth of the Pre-School Child.* New York: The Macmillan Co., 1925.

Guilford, J. P. *On the Nature of Human Intelligence.* New York: McGraw-Hill, 1967.

Harper, R. J. C.; Anderson, C. C.; Christensen, C. M.; and Hunka, S. M., eds. *The Cognitive Processes.* Englewood Cliffs, N.J.: Prentice-Hall, 1964.

Ilg, F., and Ames, L. *School Readiness.* New York: Harper & Row, Publishers, 1965.

Isaacs, S. *Intellectual Growth in Young Children.* New York: Harcourt Brace Jovanovich, 1930.

Jensen, A. R. "Learning in the Preschool Years." In *The Young Child,* edited by W. W. Hartup and N. L. Smothergill, pp. 125-35. Washington, D.C.: National Association for the Education of Young Children, 1967.

Klausmeier, H. J., and Ripple, R. E. *Learning and Human Abilities.* New York: Harper & Row, Publishers, 1971.

Piaget, J. *The Origins of Intelligence in Children.* New York: International Universities Press, 1952.

Russell, D. *Children's Thinking.* Boston: Ginn & Co., 1956.

Thompson, R. *The Psychology of Thinking.* Baltimore: Penguin Books, 1959.

Wallach, M. S., and Kogan, N. *Modes of Thinking in Young Children.* New York: Holt, Rinehart & Winston, 1965.

Wann, K. D.; Dorn, M. S.; and Liddle, E. A. *Fostering Intellectual Development in Young Children.* New York: Teachers College Press, 1962.

Perceptual and Motor Development

Arnheim, R. *Art and Visual Perception.* Berkeley: University of California Press, 1965.

_____.*Visual Thinking.* Berkeley: University of California Press, 1969.

Bruner, J. S. "On Perceptual Readiness." *Psychological Review* 64 (1957): 123-52.

Cratty, B. *Perceptual and Motor Development of Infants and Children.* New York: The Macmillan Co., 1970.

_____. *Active Learning.* Englewood Cliffs, N.J.: Prentice-Hall, 1971.

Engstrom, G. *The Significance of the Young Child's Motor Development.* Washington, D.C.: National Association for the Education of Young Children, 1971.

Fantz, R. L. "Pattern Vision in New-born Infants." *Science* 140 (April 19, 1963): 296-97.

_____. "Visual Perception from Birth as Shown by Pattern Selectivity." *Annals of the New York Academy of Sciences* 118 (1965): 793-814.

Forgus, R. H. *Perception.* New York: McGraw-Hill, 1966.

Gibson, E. J. *Perceptual Learning.* Englewood Cliffs, N.J.: Prentice-Hall, 1969.

_____. "The Development of Perception as an Adaptive Process." *American Scientist* 58 (1970): 98-107.

Kagan, J. "The Determinants of Attention in the Infant." *American Scientist* 58 (1970): 298-306.

Kidd, A., and Revoire, J. *Perceptual Development in Children.* New York: International Universities Press, 1966.

Liepmann, L. *Your Child's Sensory World.* Baltimore: Penguin Books, 1974.

Lowenstein, O. *The Senses.* London: Penguin Books, 1966.

Senden, M. von. *Space and Sight.* New York: The Free Press, 1960.

Spitzer, D. R., and McNerny, T. O. "Operationally Defining Visual Literacy: A Research Challenge." *Audiovisual Instruction* (September 1975): 30-31.

Vernon, M. D. *The Psychology of Perception.* Baltimore: Penguin Books, 1962.

Wolff, P. H. "The Development of Attention in Young Infants." *Annals of the New York Academy of Sciences* 118 (1965): 815-30.

Language Development

Bellugi, U., and Brown, R., eds. *The Acquisition of Language.* Chicago: University of Chicago Press, 1970.

Brown, R. *Words and Things.* New York: The Free Press, 1958.

Church, J. *Language and the Discovery of Reality.* New York: Vintage Books, 1966.

Lenneberg, E., ed. *The Biological Foundations of Language.* New York: John Wiley & Sons, 1967.

McCarthy, D. *The Language Development of the Preschool Child.* Minneapolis, Minn.: The University of Minnesota Press, 1930.

Piaget, J. *The Language and Thought of the Child.* London: Routledge and Kegan Paul, 1952.

Sapir, E. *Language.* New York: Harcourt Brace Jovanovich, 1921.

Vygotsky, L. S. *Thought and Language.* Cambridge, Mass.: M.I.T. Press, 1962.

Wolff, P. H. "The Natural History of Crying and Other Vocalizations in Early Infancy." In *Determinants of Infant Behavior IV,* edited by B. M. Foss, pp. 81-109. London: Methuen Publishing Co., 1969.

Motivation

Atkinson, J. W. "Motivational Determinants of Risk Taking Behavior." *Psychological Review* 64 (1957): 359-72.

Bandura, A. "Social Learning Through Imitation." In *Nebraska Symposium on Motivation, 1962,* edited by M. R. Jones, pp. 211-69. Lincoln: University of Nebraska Press, 1962.

Deci, E. L. "Effects of Externally Mediated Reward on Intrinsic Motivation." *Journal of Personality and Social Psychology* 18 (1971): 105-15.

Hill, W. F. "Activity as an Autonomous Drive." *Journal of Comparative Physiological Psychology* 49 (1956): 15-19.

Horowitz, F. "Incentive Value of Social Stimuli for Preschool Children." *Child Development* 35 (1962): 111-16.

Hunt, J. McV. "Motivation Inherent in Information Processing and Action." In *Motivation and Social Interaction,* edited by O. J. Harvey, pp. 35-94. New York: The Ronald Press Co., 1963.

Leuba, C. "Toward Some Integration of Learning Theories: The Concept of Optimal Stimulation." *Psychological Reports* 1 (1955): 27-33.

McClelland, D. C. "Toward a Theory of Motive Acquisition." *American Psychologist* 20 (1965): 321-33.

_____. *The Achieving Society.* New York: The Free Press, 1967.

Maslow, A. *Motivation and Personality.* New York: Harper & Row, Publishers, 1970.

Murray, H. A. *Explorations in Personality.* New York: Oxford University Press, 1938.

Seligman, M. E. P. *Helplessness.* San Francisco: W. H. Freeman & Co., 1974.

Thompson, W. R. "Motivational Factors in Development." *Australian Journal of Psychology* 10 (1958): 127-43.

Weiner, B. *Theories of Motivation.* Chicago: Markham Publishing Co., 1972.

White, R. W. "Motivation Reconsidered: The Concept of Competence." *Psychological Review* 66 (1959): 297-333.

Wolff, P. H. "Developmental and Motivational Concepts in Piaget's Sensorimotor Theory of Intelligence." *Journal of the American Academy of Child Psychiatry* 2 (1963): 225-43.

Instructional Practices

Almy, M. *The Early Childhood Educator at Work.* New York: McGraw-Hill, 1975.

Bloom, B. S. "Early Learning in the Home." Paper presented at the University of California, Los Angeles, July 18, 1965. ERIC document ED–019–127.

Bruner, J. S. *Toward a Theory of Instruction.* Cambridge, Mass.: The Belknap Press, 1967.

Gagné, R. M. *The Conditions of Learning.* New York: Holt, Rinehart & Winston, 1970.

Gattegno, C. *Toward a Visual Culture.* New York: Outersbridge and Dienstfrey, 1969.

_____. *What We Owe Children.* New York: Avon Books, 1970.

Hess, R. D., and Croft, D. *Teachers of Young Children.* New York: Houghton Mifflin Co., 1972.

Mathis, B. C.; Cotton, J. W.; and Sechrest, L. *Psychological Foundations of Education.* New York: The Academic Press, 1970.

Palmer, E. L. "Sesame Street: Shaping Broadcast Television to Needs of the Preschooler." *Educational Technology,* February 1971, pp. 18-22.

Pavlov, I. P. *Conditioned Reflexes.* London: Oxford University Press, 1927.

_____. *Lectures on Conditioned Reflexes.* New York: International Publishers, 1928.

Pines, M. *Revolution in Learning.* New York: Harper & Row, Publishers, 1966.

Sapir, S. G., and Nitzburg, A. C. *Children With Learning Problems.* New York: Brunner/Mazel, Publishers, 1973.

Skinner, B. F. *The Behavior of Organisms.* New York: Appleton-Century-Crofts, 1938.

_____. "Teaching Machines." *Science* 128 (1958): 969-77.

_____. *The Technology of Teaching.* New York: Appleton-Century-Crofts, 1968.

Tyler, F. T. "Issues Related to Readiness." In *Sixty-third Yearbook, National Society for the Study of Education,* Vol. 2 edited by D. E. Griffith, pp. 210-39. Chicago: University of Chicago Press, 1964.

Woodruff, A. D. "Cognitive Models of Learning and Instruction." In *Instruction: Some Contemporary Viewpoints,* edited by L. Siegel, pp. 55-98. San Francisco: Chandler Publishing Co., 1967.

Creativity and Play

Abt, C. C. *Serious Games,* New York: The Viking Press, 1970.

Almy, M. "Spontaneous Play: An Avenue for Intellectual Development." *Young Children* 22 (May 1967): 265-77.

Barron, F. "The Disposition Toward Originality." *Journal of Abnormal and Social Psychology* 51 (1955): 478-85.

Caplan, F., and Caplan, T. *The Power of Play.* New York: Anchor Books, 1974.

Di Leo, J. H. *Young Children and Their Drawings.* New York: Brunner/Mazel, Publishers, 1970.

Getzels, J. W., and Jackson, P. W. *Creativity and Intelligence.* New York: John Wiley & Sons, 1962.

Ghiselin, B. *The Creative Process.* Berkeley: University of California Press, 1952.

Hartley, R. E.; Frank, L. K.; and Goldenson, R. M. *Understanding Children's Play.* New York: Columbia University Press, 1952.

Koestler, A. *The Act of Creation.* New York: The Macmillan Co., 1964.

Lowenfeld, V. *Creative and Mental Growth.* New York: The Macmillan Co., 1957.

_____. *Play in Childhood.* New York: John Wiley & Sons, 1967.

Torrance, P. "Factors Affecting Creative Thinking in Children," *Merrill-Palmer Quarterly* 7 (1961): 171-80.

Vygotsky, L. S. "Play and Its Role in the Mental Development of the Child." *Soviet Psychology* 12 (1966): 6-17.

Wallach, M. A. "Creativity and the Expression of Possibilities." In *Creativity and Learning,* edited by J. Kagan, pp. 36-57. Boston: Houghton Mifflin Co., 1967.

Young, M. A. *Buttons Are To Push.* New York: Pitman Publishing Corp., 1970.

General Resources

Ausubel, D. P., and Sullivan, E. V. *Theory and Problems of Child Development.* New York: Grune & Stratton, 1970.

Baldwin, A. *Behavior and Development in Childhood.* New York: The Dreyden Press, 1955.

Bloom, B. S. *Stability and Change in Human Characteristics.* New York: John Wiley & Sons, 1964.

Braga, J., and Braga, L. *Growing With Children.* Englewood Cliffs, N.J.: Prentice-Hall, 1974.

_____. *Learning and Growing.* Englewood Cliffs, N.J.: Prentice-Hall, 1975.

Buhler, C. *The First Year of Life.* New York: John Day Co., 1930.

Butler, A. L. *Current Research in Early Childhood Education.* Washington, D.C.: American Association of Elementary-Kindergarten-Nursery Educators, 1970.

Carmichael, L., ed. *Manual of Child Psychology.* New York: John Wiley & Sons, 1946.

Crow, L. D., and Crow, A. *Child Development and Adjustment.* New York: The Macmillan Co., 1962.

Elkind, D. *Children and Adolescents: Interpretive Essays on Jean Piaget.* New York: Oxford University Press, 1974.

Erikson, E. H. *Childhood and Society.* New York: W. W. Norton and Company, 1950.

Fraiberg, S. H. *The Magic Years.* New York: Charles Scribners' Sons, 1959.

Frost, J. L., ed. *Early Childhood Education Rediscovered, Readings.* New York: Holt, Rinehart & Winston, 1968.

Gesell, A. *Infancy and Human Growth.* New York: The Macmillan Co., 1928.

Gesell, A., and Ilg, F. *Infant and Child in the Culture of Today.* New York: Harper & Row, Publishers, 1943.

Hartup, W. W., and Smothergill, N. L., eds. *The Young Child*. Washington, D.C.: National Association for the Education of Young Children, 1970.

Hebb, D. O. *The Organization of Behavior*. New York: John Wiley & Sons, 1949.

Hess, R. D., and Bear, R. M., eds. *Early Education*. Chicago: Aldine Publishing Co., 1968.

Hunt, J. McV. *Intelligence and Experience*. New York: The Ronald Press Co., 1961.

Inhelder, B., and Piaget, J. *The Growth of Logical Thinking from Childhood to Adolescence. New York: Basic Books, 1958.*

_____. *The Psychology of the Child*. New York: Basic Books, 1969.

Jersild, A. T. *Child Psychology*. Englewood Cliffs, N.J.: Prentice-Hall, 1960.

Lewis, M. *Language, Thought and Personality in Infancy and Childhood*. New York: Basic Books, 1963.

Montessori, M. *Dr. Montessori's Own Handbook*. New York: Schocken Books, 1965.

_____. *The Discovery of the Child*. New York: Ballantine Books, 1967.

_____. *The Absorbent Mind*. New York: Holt, Rinehart & Winston, 1967.

Muller, P. *The Tasks of Childhood*. New York: McGraw-Hill, 1969.

Piaget, J. *The Child's Conception of the World*. New York: Harcourt Brace Jovanovich, 1929.

_____. *The Construction of Reality in the Child*. New York: Basic Books, 1954.

_____. *The Moral Judgment of the Child*. Glencoe, Ill.: The Free Press, 1948.

_____. *Play, Dreams and Imitation in Childhood*. New York: W. W. Norton and Co., 1951.

_____. *The Psychology of Intelligence*. New York: Harcourt Brace Jovanovich, 1950.

Piaget, J., and Inhelder, B. *The Child's Conception of Space*. London: Routledge and Kegan Paul, 1956.

_____. *The Early Growth of Logic in the Child*. New York: Harper & Row, Publishers, 1964.

Sears, R.; Maccoby, E.; and Levin, H. *Patterns of Child Rearing*. New York: Harper & Row, Publishers, 1957.

Sharp, E. *Thinking is Child's Play*. New York: E. P. Dutton and Co., 1969.

Spitzer, D. R. "What Is a Concept?" *Educational Technology,* July 1975, pp. 36-39.

Stevenson, H. W. *Television and the Behavior of Preschool Children*. Minneapolis, Minn.: University of Minnesota Press, 1971.

Stone, L. J.; Smith, H. T.; and Murphy, L. B., eds. *The Competent Infant*. New York: Basic Books, 1973.

Vincent, E., and Martin, P. *Human Psychological Development.* New York: The Ronald Press Co., 1961.

Watson, R. *Psychology of the Child.* New York: John Wiley & Sons, 1973.

White, B. L. "Child Development Research: An Edifice without a Foundation." *Merrill-Palmer Quarterly* 15 (1969): 49-79.

_____. *Human Infants: Experience and Psychological Development.* Englewood Cliffs, N.J.: Prentice-Hall, 1971.

Index

Accommodation, 17, 19, 29, 105
Accountability, 80
Action for Children's Television, 13
Aesthetic appreciation, 123
Ames, Louise, 9
Arnheim, Rudolf, 67, 70
Assimilation, 17, 29, 79, 105
Association, 29–31, 35, 39, 43, 49, 120
Attention, 66, 67, 105, 120
Attention span, 58–59, 76, 135

Bayley, Nancy, 9
Bereiter-Englemann program, 8, 11
Berlyne, Daniel, 57, 92, 94
Bloom, Benjamin, 9, 12, 55
Bruner, Jerome, 9, 35, 75

Collections, 42, 45
Comparison, 68, 69–70, 126, 128, 145
Competence, 5, 32, 34–35, 63, 80, 94,
    96, 98, 128
  play, 75, 76
  effectance, 86
  self-effectiveness, 144
Completion, 68–69
Complexes, 42–43
  associative, 44–45
  chain, 45
  diffuse, 45
Complexity, 57–58, 95, 96, 98
Concepts, 5, 23–28, 54, 98
  concrete, 7
  of early childhood, 3, 62

(Concepts continued)
  external, 24–25, 44
  formation of, 6, 21, 23, 24–28, 36–40,
    41–48, 60–62, 107
  internal, 24–25
  limitations, 25
  visual, 66–71
Conceptualization, 25, 26, 42, 66, 67
Concrete-operational stage, 18
Conditioned learning, 29–31
Conservation, 22, 128
Context interpretation, 68, 70
Convergent production, 82–83
Creativity, 82–91, 101, 116, 127, 139,
    142, 148
  convergent production, 82–83
  divergent production, 82–83
  flexibility, 83, 84, 85
  independence, 83, 84–85
  originality, 83, 85
  playfulness, 83, 85
  venturesomeness, 83, 84, 85
Curiosity, 14, 50, 52, 73, 84, 96, 100, 133

Day care centers, 8
Developmental approach, 3
Developmental psychologists, 29
Developmental tasks, 4
Di Leo, J. H., 87–88, 89
Discrimination, 36, 38, 39, 120, 121,
    126, 147
Divergent production, 82–83

Early childhood education, 2, 7, 8, 10, 11, 98, 101
Educational television, 12–13
  influences, 13
Effectance, 86
Esteem, 78
Evaluation of development, 80–81
Expectancies, 94–95

Fantasy, 73–74
Fantz, 9, 58
Flexibility, 83, 84, 85, 139
Follow Through program, 8
Formal-operational stage, 18

Gattegno, Caleb, 14
Generalization, 35, 38, 39
  response, 35
  stimulus, 35
Gesell, Arnold, 9
Getzels, J. W., 91
Gibson, Eleanor, 9
Gordon, Ira, 9
Graphic collections, 43, 46–47
  collective alignments, 46
  collective objects, 46–47
  complex objects, 47
Guilford, J. P., 82, 83, 91

Head Start, 8, 10, 11
Heaps, 41, 42–43
Hebb, Donald, 9, 57, 92, 94
Higher-level learning, 36–40
Hill, W. F., 94
Home Start program, 8
Hunt, J. McV., 9, 11–12

Imitation, 20
Incentives, 95–96
Incidental learning, 31
Independence, 83, 84–85
Inhelder, Barbel, 41
Institute for Developmental Studies, 11
Intellectual abilities, 3, 16, 55, 98
Intelligence, 16
  creativity and, 91
  I.Q. scores, 11, 55

Jackson, Phillip, 91
Journals, early childhood, 9

Kagan, Jerome, 9
Kogan, Nathan, 91

Language acquisition, 4, 6, 7, 21, 26–28, 89–90, 103
  early speech, 53–54
Learned helplessness, 34

Learning deficiencies, 11
Learning theories, 29–40
Lewin, Kurt, 2
Lowenfeld, Viktor, 87–88

Manipulation, 3, 6, 51, 63, 88, 101, 105, 107, 108, 112, 114, 116, 120, 127
Maslow, Abraham, 93
Maturation, 4, 59
Meaning, 27–28, 43
  hidden, 27–28
Memory, 64–65
  recall, 65
  recognition, 65, 113, 122, 147
  recollection, 65
Montessori, Maria, 8, 9, 34–35, 79, 81
Motivation, 5, 33, 66, 75, 78–79, 92–96, 125
  achievement motivation, 84
  competence motivation, 5
  incentives, 95–96
  intrinsic motivation, 92–94
  motives, 94–96
Motor abilities, 3, 62–64, 88, 97, 105, 110, 111–12, 131, 132, 135, 144, 147
Murphy, Lois, 9

Nongraphic collections, 47–48
Novelty, 57–58, 64, 73, 76, 95, 98

Object permanence, 19, 20, 51, 53, 59–60, 113–14
Organization of experience, 3, 5, 25–28, 38, 40
Organizations, early childhood, 10
Originality, 83, 85

Pavlov, Ivan, 30, 38
Perception, 3, 4, 6, 56–62
  perceptual abilities, 3, 12, 15, 32, 58–60, 62, 97, 108, 110, 120, 121
  perceptual constancies, 60, 116
  perceptual differentiation, 59
  perceptual difficulties, 103
  perceptual flexibility, 59
  perceptual selectivity, 60–61
Perry Preschool Project, 11
Piaget, Jean, 9, 12, 29, 49, 50, 84, 105, 128
  theories, 17–22, 41–43, 46–48
Pines, Maya, 10, 11
Play, 72–77, 85, 102
  problem-solving and, 74–75
  self-discipline in, 75
  symbolic play, 20
Playfulness, 83, 85

Practice, 102, 114, 126, 145
Preoperational stage, 20–22
Preschool programs, 7, 10–12
Pseudo-concepts, 45–46
Punishment, 34

Readiness, 5, 64, 97, 103
Reinforcement, 30, 93–94
Response strength, 31

Selection, 68, 69
Self-concept, 5, 63, 81, 134, 146, 147
Self-esteem, 78, 79, 146
Self-evaluation, 80
Senses, 4, 6, 56–62
    sensory learning, 4, 28, 51–52, 64,
    115–16
Sensorimotor stage, 18, 19–20, 51
Sesame Street, 8, 12–13
Simplification, 68–69
Skinner, B. F., 33
Social learning, 4, 13
    from television, 13
Spitz, Rene, 9
*Stability and Change in Human Characteris-
    tics,* 12
Stimulation, early, 3, 4, 15, 26–27, 49–52,
    53, 54, 104–5
Stages of development, 16, 18–22
Sucking response, 110

Successive approximation, 32–34

Thought and Language, 43
Torrance, Paul, 54
Toward a Visual Culture, 14
Toys and games, 28
    educational, 14
Trial-and-error, 31–32, 113

Variety, 51–52
Venturesomeness, 83, 84, 85
Vicarious experience, 3, 14, 93
Vision, 4, 6, 56–62
    attention, 50, 66
    fixation, 66, 67
    visual acuity, 57, 88, 107, 131, 138
    visual exploration, 66, 67, 107, 108,
    136
    visual learning, 14, 15, 108
    visual search, 66, 67, 109
Vygotsky, Lev, 9, 75
    theory, 41–46

Wallach, Michael, 91
War on Poverty, 10
White, Burton, 9
White, Robert, 92, 94
Wolff, Peter, 9
Woodruff, A. D., 64

Young, Milton, 54